TAKING A LESSON FROM THE MISTAKES OF OTHERS

S. C. SAWHNEY

UNIVERSITY SCIENCE PRESS

(An Imprint of Laxmi Publications Pvt. Ltd.)

BANGALORE ● CHENNAI ● COCHIN ● GUWAHATI ● HYDERABAD
JALANDHAR ● KOLKATA ● LUCKNOW ● MUMBAI ● PATNA
RANCHI ● NEW DELHI

Published by

UNIVERSITY SCIENCE PRESS

(*An Imprint of Laxmi Publications Pvt. Ltd.*)

113, Golden House, Daryaganj,

New Delhi-110 002

Phone: 011-43 53 25 00

Fax: 011-43 53 25 28

www.laxmipublications.com

info@laxmipublications.com

First Edition 2012

OFFICES

Bangalore	080-26 75 69 30	**Chennai**	044-24 34 47 26
Cochin	0484-237 70 04, 405 13 03	**Guwahati**	0361-251 36 69, 251 38 81
Hyderabad	040-24 65 23 33	**Jalandhar**	0181-222 12 72
Kolkata	033-22 27 43 84	**Lucknow**	0522-220 99 16
Mumbai	022-24 91 54 15, 24 92 78 69	**Patna**	0612-230 00 97
Ranchi	0651-221 47 64		

UTL-9650-080-TAKE LESSON MIS OTH-SAW **C—4026/011/09**

Typeset at Sukuvisa Enterprises, Delhi *Printed at* Repro Knowledgecast Limited, Thane

TAKING A LESSON FROM THE MISTAKES OF OTHERS

PREFACE

Doing something objectionable to the society is generally regarded a mistake. Doing something not permitted under law is considered a crime. Similarly, doing something not permitted under the religion is considered a sin. Whether we commit a mistake, a crime, or a sin, we stand to lose not only our reputation and incur some financial loss, but we may also have some mental distress. Unless we are able to satisfy others that we are right we can't claim to be right.

Yet we may also have to do some things that are normally not permitted, due to some reasons of our own. But as long as we are not expected to compensate for the loss anybody may incur due to such an action and we don't compensate the affected person, we would be considered to have committed a mistake.

If we ever commit a mistake it only shows that we had not been as cautious as we should have been. Of course, the mistakes make us more cautious for the future. But it is not enough to depend only on our own mistakes. We should also learn lessons from the mistakes committed by others. The following quotation of "*Chicago Tribune*" inspires us to develop the habit of making the mistakes of other persons also a ground for learning.

> *Only some of us can learn by other people's mistakes. The rest of us have to be the other people.*

The quotation does not speak well of the people who do not learn from the mistakes of others.

This book begins with the story of a girl who reposed too much confidence in her inner voice. She married a boy without even ascertaining his family background. No wonder, it became too late by the time she could realize that our inner voice can mislead us also. This way, I have covered several real-life stories to make you aware of the type of mistakes some people have committed in their life. I have, however, also focused on the action these persons took to rebuild their image.

The book is of course neither a treatise of all types of mistakes nor I expect that you too would pass through the situations these persons had passed. But I expect that whatever types of situations you may pass through, these examples would go a long way to let you take a right decision in your future life.

—Author

ACKNOWLEDGEMENTS

There are some persons who always try to do something that may give pleasure to others. They like to ascertain what help they can render to others to make them feel happy. I think Ram Tirath Mohan who had come to Lucknow, his native place from abroad after retirement from his service in the Foreign Services of India is also a man of this type. I know him only as a neighbour who gifted me a set of the books of the Chicken Soup series when he found that I had not read them yet. After reading these books I felt like writing a book which could help people lead a better life. I feel grateful to him for having gifted these books because I would not have written this book had he not gifted me this set of books.

I am particularly thankful to my daughter Dr. Jyotsna Mehta who depite her very tight schedule spared her time to go through the book to give her views about it.

I am also thankful to P.C. Gupta who was my senior at Scooters India Limited, Lucknow for having provided me a list of publishers whom I could contact to publish the book.

CONTENTS

1 Story of a Young Girl who Ruined Her Life by Marrying a Wrong Boy

Since we have no mechanism to know what type of life we would be leading after marriage we generally base our decision of marriage only on a hunch. If we feel the person whom we like would be able to keep us happy, we give our consent to marry him or her. But because when we marry we tie our life with the life of the other person we should not give our consent without taking even some basic precautions such as verification of the family background and the academic qualifications of the person.

This story relates to a girl who did not bother to verify the credentials of the boy prior to her marriage. She simply trusted her inner voice and decided to marry a boy who turned out to be just a vagabond eventually. This story had been displayed on TV on 4th August 2007 by the Star News Channel.

The story tells us that our inner voice can mislead us. We may listen to the inner voice but not blindly. The girls in particular should check the background of the boy they may intend to marry if they don't want to ruin their life. They should remember that to be in love is not enough for a happy marriage. Such marriage may not turn out to be a happy marriage necessarily. So if their parents had taken enough interest in their upbringing, they should take them in confidence while making a judgment about the boy they may like to marry, as so many boys only want to have some gay time for themselves till they get married to a girl selected by their parents.

Many girls repose too much confidence on their boy friends. But even they sometimes cheat them. Girls in the Indian families are not exposed to the type of people they can come across in life because their parents provide them much more protection than to their sons. So they are more liable to get trapped in a group of antisocial type of people.

Development of judgment in dealing with different types of persons in life is just like soaking our feet in the water of a swimming pool before jumping into it. This practice only tells us, it is necessary to take precautions in life. This girl did not take necessary precautions before she decided to marry the boy of whom she thought was a boy designated by her destiny.

Till the girls develop full confidence, it is safer for them to listen to their parents instead of bypassing or sidelining them. They should remember that their parents have more worldly experience than them. So they should take the benefit of their experience at least in such matters as the choice of the groom for themselves. Those who don't think so are liable to commit a mistake of the type this girl had committed. Decision of marriage is not a decision that should be taken in such haste as this girl had taken.

For a decision like marriage, the girls in particular have to be more cautious because a wrong decision can shatter their rest of life because particularly in India, it becomes very difficult to find a good match for the girls who may have been divorced or who may have become victims of some blemishing incident.

Girls generally ignore their parents only when they take extraordinarily long time to let them take independent decisions. In such cases they lose their patience and try to go ahead without taking them in confidence.

Only the parents of the girls, who don't have any financial means other than what their daughter may provide, delay the marriage of their daughters out of selfishness. So such girls often, out of frustration, try to look for some boy who may be willing to marry them.

No doubt a girl can take a decision about her marriage herself but not in a manner this girl had taken.

This girl was quite a bright student of a prestigious college of Delhi. One day, when she was returning from the college, her foot hit a boulder that had been kept on the road by the Municipal Corporation people and she fell down on the road. She got so badly hurt that she could not even get up without the help of a boy who was looking at the incident and had come to her help. He offered to even drop her at her house on his motorbike. Though initially reluctant, she thought that perhaps God had sent him to help her at a time when she was not able to even walk. So she gave her consent. When they reached her home, she thanked him for having helped her. But later on she kept on thinking about the incident and could not resist thinking why she had not even asked his name. The boy had also not asked her name.

It so happened that the girl once again met the same boy and asked him why he had helped her when she had hit the stone the other day. This boy was actually not at all a good boy. He was in a group of the people who traded girls for money in the flesh trade. But the girl thought the other way. She thought that she was being guided by her destiny. So she proposed to marry him and the boy agreed to her proposal also. She didn't ask him about his family background or his educational qualifications even. She assumed that he must be belonging to a good family only or else why should he have come forward to help her when she had struck the boulder. But when she narrated the story to her parents and told them that she wanted to marry the boy, they did not give their consent. Hindus give lot of consideration to the family background of the prospective grooms and the brides when they decide about the marriage of their children. But the girl was so firm about her decision that she, one day left the home and went ahead to marry the boy in a temple. Neither the boy nor the girl thought it necessary to invite anyone to their marriage. They silently married in a temple.

But within a few days of the marriage, the boy planned to sell off the girl. So he took her to the *Mandi* where the girls are sold for a price. Even though some policemen told the girl that she perhaps was not aware that the boy had brought her there only to sell her. They even arrested the boy. But when the boy requested the girl that she should save him, she obliged him thinking that now he will not repeat such mistake again. But the boy again fixed a deal with a party of Himachal Pradesh and took her to a place in Himachal Pradesh telling her that there he could get her a job. But instead of getting her a job, he sold her to a group of boys where she was gang-raped by as many as twenty-six boys in a row. She somehow managed to escape from their trap. But on her way, she met a man who promised to help her. However to her bad luck, he too sold her to a group of people who were in the same trade of buying and selling the girls. Fed up with her life she contacted her parents to tell them what had happened. But they refused to accept her because she had not paid any heed to their advice. What happened afterwards is not known.

Should we say, it all happened in her life only because she had bad stars?

It is said that whenever we may be in some confusion, we should listen to our inner voice. This girl had also listened to her inner voice. But why did she still marry him? M. Henry's following quotation gives us an answer.

"When passion is on the throne, reason is out of doors."

So her inner voice got muffed and her power of judgment got blurred due to the passion. What happened in her life would have not happened, had she listened to her parents or she would have enquired the boy about his family background. What lesson can we take from this story? The lesson is clear. Young girls should value the opinion of their parents in respect of marriage instead of losing their sense out of passion.

No well-intentioned parent ever likes that his or her daughter should marry a person who would not keep her happy. If the girls are sure that their parents are well-intentioned they should have patience till they find a good match for them. Though even well-intentioned parents also sometimes fail in making right judgment, they are less likely to commit mistakes than their children.

Our inner voice can quite sometimes mislead us too. In one case near Lucknow a retired army man dreamt one day that he should construct a temple of Lord Venkateshwara on his farm.

So he built a huge temple on his farm. But he did not think that the people of Lucknow don't worship Lord Venkateshwara as they worship other deities. He realized his mistake only when he saw that no body ever came to the temple for several years. So we should not act on our inner voice in an indiscreet manner.

If the parents think they can't find a good match for their children they often ask the children to find out a match of their choice themselves and introduce the groom or the bride to them, when they come across some one whom they may intend to marry. But even if they select a match themselves, they should take the opinion of the parents and get the proposal approved.

2 *Story of the Families of Gladys Rozin and Barry Fisher*

This is a real story which tells us how under similar circumstances, one family got ruined while the other family didn't. Obviously the family that got ruined didn't know how to handle the crisis, while the other family knew. This case had been narrated by Morton Hunt in his article, "Is Your Family Crisis-Proof?" which I picked up from the book "Happy Families", published in 1989 by Reader's Digest. Through this case study, Hunt had described how we can survive if we take help of the friends, when in some crisis.

In this article, he has told that one fall day, a lady Mrs. Gladys Rozin saw a boy zooming down a side street on his skateboard when she was driving home at dusk planning dinner for her family and felt a terrible thump and a minute later heard her own scream. The boy had been run over by her car. In the same story, he also told about a man Barry Fisher who on a rainy day, in a similar suburb, was hurrying home after work to tell his wife and two teen-agers, about his promotion. Squinting into a downpour, he jammed on the brakes when he suddenly saw a man in the road changing a flat tyre. He knew, as the car skidded, that there was no hope. It was also a case of accidental homicide, in which both the boy and the man died. A homicide of this type is not just a tragedy for the family of the victim but for the family of the one, who commits it also. But Hunt told how, while the Rozin family disintegrated within two years the other family did not.

Hunt has told in the story, how the Rozins tried to avoid the dreadful subject and ended up avoiding one another. For months they shunned friends, and finally moved where no one knew their story. She became an insomniac and an alcoholic. Her both children faced difficulties in school and her husband, George Rozin got involved with another woman. But in case of Fishers, though Barry's wife and children, suffered with him, they believed in him and clung to him. They reached out to their friends and relatives for support. While the insurance covered a part of settlement worked out by their lawyers, both Barry and his wife went back to work and paid off the balance amount without having to sell their house.

This example tells us that in this world, we can survive a crisis of this type by taking help of each other. A person, who feels that no one is going to help him, meets the fate of the family of Gladys Rozin. But one who takes others into confidence and solicits the help of others is able to return to the normal life after the ordeal is over like Fishers.

Not only such accidents, there can be many other situations also that can be successfully dealt with if we don't lose the balance of our mind and remain composed through out the crisis. This helps us to plan a correct strategy for each crisis.

Some parents may get shocked when they may discover that their unwed daughter got pregnant with the tutor they had engaged for her tuition at the home of the tutor or at their own home or if she may elope with some boy-friend. Out of shock, some parents even decide to kill or disown their daughter forgetting that such a situation could have not arisen had they been a little more vigilant. Actually they themselves are to be blamed for not having been vigilant. So they should not punish their daughter in such cases. Just imagine how shocking would it be for a daughter to see that she is being killed or burnt alive by none else but her own father or mother. We have to take a wise step under such cases instead of taking a rash action for which police may arrest us for interrogation or for which we may have to repent, later, for whole of our life. If we act wisely, our children would also learn how to handle a crisis. It is better to let the children learn how to get out of a crisis instead of killing them or leaving them at a lonely place to fend for themselves.

It is seen that with the changing life patterns nowadays many children don't show much of interest in taking care of their ailing parents in their old age. The problem arises when the children may tell them to live with each of them for a few months by rotation or they may ask one of the parents to live with one of them and the other parent with the other one. The parents, who may not have enough money to make their own arrangements in the old age, find it very humiliating to live in this manner. Even the children who are not short of money sometimes don't want their parents to live with them under the same roof. In such cases some parents decide to move to some charitable old age home. But when the children don't heed to even visit them in the old age homes, they pass through great mental stress. We can avoid this type of crisis by planning for a permanent source of income in the old age.

Besides having an arrangement of this type, the parents have to also look for the reasons of such an attitude of the children. They have to, for instance, remember that they can no longer continue to be as authoritative in the family as they may have been when their children were still unmarried. Another reason may be their too much interference in their personal lives. So in old age we have to adapt ourselves a lot to live with the children without making much fuss.

Children may also not like their parents to have extramarital relations. They generally don't tolerate their father to have illicit relations with some other woman or the mother to have illicit relations with some other man. They know what impact such illicit relations may have on their children.

Even otherwise mutual trust is the foundation of a successful marriage. Both the husband and wife expect that their partner does not develop extramarital relationships. Husbands in particular do not tolerate infidelity of the wives. So by having illicit relations we create a crisis in our life ourselves. No wonder, the children may also go into shock if they come to know that their parents have frank extramarital relations with someone. If so, they can't be blamed for not allowing their parents to live with them. How can they tolerate that the parents themselves do not uphold the values they had tried to build in them all their life? How can we set a different standard for ourselves than for the children?

Sometimes old parents expect their children to give them lot more attention than it may at all be possible for them. So quite often, we ourselves become responsible for becoming incompatible to live together with our children in the old age.

3 Story of Hindi Poet Tulsidas

What we achieve in our life depends to a good extent on the way we react to various ugly situations that may arise in our life. Here is a story that tells us how.

The story of the great Hindi poet Tulsidas tells us how we can change our whole life by not reacting in a Tit-For-Tat way when we may commit some shameful mistake. We remember Tulsidas more for the several books he had written, more so for his "Ram Charit Manas". But we should actually remember him better for the way he changed his life instead of getting offended when he had climbed to the attic of her beloved using a snake as a rope.

In normal course he would have perhaps never written such a book at all. It was this woman who turned his attention toward this side. This woman was the one whom he used to intensely love. He used to think that she too loved him with the same intensity.

As the story goes, it is said, one night when it was raining cats and dogs, Tulsidas decided to visit his sweetheart, who used to live in an attic. When he reached her house, he could not even notice that a snake was hanging outside her house. He thought that his beloved had hung a rope especially for him so that he could climb up to her attic. So he climbed up to her attic by holding the snake and thanked the lady for having made this arrangement for him.

The lady got surprised when he thanked her because she had not hung any rope to let him climb to her attic. So they both went out to see the rope and were shocked to see that what Tulsidas had described as rope, was actually a snake, not a rope. Tulsidas felt very ashamed of himself for not having been able to even discern a snake from a rope. He felt ashamed to his skin because the lady told him to devout to God rather than paying so much attention to a mortal being like her. Her remarks hurt him so much that he stopped going to her thereafter. But he used to feel very ashamed when his friends started making fun of him for his having been spurned by the lady.

He kept on thinking how he could earn respect of the people instead of having become a laughing stock. So he started reading the life history of Lord Rama and finally decided to write Rama's life in a manner that it has become a Bible for the Hindus.

Though initially he was at a loss to think what the people would think of him, he eventually found this unique way to change their opinion about him. He didn't go into depression nor did he lose the balance of his mind. Instead, he used his creative energy in a manner that people hold him in great regard even today. Even the next generations would pay homage to him for the extraordinary contribution he made by writing this book.

This incident churned up his inner sensibilities to such an extent that he became an immortal poet after this incident. We may say, the entire credit goes to this incident only? Not, exactly. Actually what made him an immortal poet was, his reaction to the incident.

So we should never feel sad if an incident that we may make us feel ashamed may occur in our life. All we have to do is, to divert our energies toward a cause that may immortalize us as Tulsidas had done.

We may also give some credit for this lady because it was she who prompted him to dedicate himself to God instead of her.

It is said, behind every successful man there is some woman. She may not necessarily be our beloved. She can be even our mother, sister or a friend or some other woman. She may be even our wife. In the same way, quite often there is some man behind the success of a woman also. At some stage or another, our destiny brings some man or woman close to us who gets inclined to help us or inspire us to write our success story.

Just see, how even a shock can sometimes turn into a blessing. So we should never be afraid of getting shocks. These shocks can change our life as had happened in case of Tulsidas. It's not that he did not retaliate. He retaliated but in quite a different way.

4 *Story of the Great Sanskrit Poet Kalidas*

Kalidas is known for having been found sitting on the exterior side of a branch of a tree while cutting it with his axe by the pundits who were on a look out for a man about whom they wanted to convince the ablest lady of those days to be the most eligible young man she could find for her marriage. The name of this lady was Vidyuttama and she used to always defeat all the male pundits in various religious discussions due to her superior knowledge. The male pundits considered it a matter of great shame and annoyance for them that a lady should defeat them in all the discourses. So, out of revenge, they decided to look for a foolish type of young boy about whom they could convince this lady that he was the most learned man of the country so that she may get ready to marry him.

It is this young man who later on wrote the great masterpieces "Meghdoot" and "Abhigyan Shakuntalam" even though he was an unlettered man at the time of his marriage.

With this plan, they went out in search of some such lad and selected Kalidas for this purpose when they saw him sitting on a branch of a tree trying to cut it with his axe unaware of the fact that he should have not been sitting on the exterior side of the branch while trying to cut it. This boy was totally illiterate and did not know a word of Sanskrit. So they selected this boy and told him that they would get him married to one of the most learned lady of the country provided he agreed to remain silent when they talked to this lady about this proposal.

They told him to answer her questions only through body language. The boy agreed to their tempting proposal. When they took him to the lady they told the lady that the boy they had brought to her was a highly learned pundit but had kept "*Mauni Vrat*" since last month. This is a type of fast, pundits used to observe during which they used to restrain themselves from talking to people for a period ranging from one day to a few months, so that they could carry out their meditation with full concentration.

When they took Kalidas to her, he answered the questions asked by her but the male pundits accompanying him, satisfied her what he meant by the physical movements of his hands and other limbs in a manner that she got convinced about his immense knowledge.

So she gave her consent to marry him. But it did not take the lady any time to discover that she had been duped by the pundits, on the first night of the marriage itself. Unable to bear the crude joke they played and the mistake she had committed, she threw Kalidas out of the window of the room where they were supposed to spend the night.

Just imagine the trauma Kalidas would have gone through. But he did not shout. Nor did he blame anyone. He simply took a vow to become more learned than this lady. What a task for an unlettered man? But he started learning Sanskrit and managed to become not just the best scholar of Sanskrit, he even became the biggest Sanskrit poet also. Till today, people marvel at his capability to express things in such a vivid manner, as he has expressed in his books.

What a unique and brilliant way of reacting to the awkward situation he had been put into! Instead of getting angry on anyone he responded to his inner consciousness that told him to take the revenge in a manner that has shown to the world that if one is illiterate it should not think that he cannot become a big scholar. He did not try to throw acid on the face of the lady as many young boys do these days when they do not respond to their advances. Nor did he try to kill any one. This explains how we can be guided by our inner consciousness if we do not try to avenge some body's ill intentions.

The insult done to him worked out as a boon to him. Such incidents actually stir us so much that we feel as if the whole world is laughing at us. Some people lose the balance of their mind. Only a few of us are able to control their senses and remain calm like Kalidas. When hurt like this, what can be better example of taking revenge than the way Kalidas had taken?

At some point of time or another we all get insulted by some body or the else. But how often do we react in the manner Kalidas had reacted? We too can try to do some thing that could stun the world.

This story shows how even a jolt we get in life can give us an opportunity to rise in life. This is the reason why we should not be afraid of the jolts. Each jolt gives us an opportunity to excel in life. It adds to our tenacity to deal with problems. First we deal with small problems and then bigger problems. The bigger problems we are able to deal with successfully, it goes on building our self-confidence.

Many times some people get shocked even for no good reason. It is understandable to get shocked if one may lose a legal fight, or may get defrauded of his entire property or when someone may withdraw lot of money from his bank account by stealing his password or by creating clones of his credit cards. It is also understandable if someone may get shocked if he gets bereaved of his most loved companion or the sole bread winner of his family when all other members may still not be in a position to earn, yet. But to get shocked when there is hardly any reason is ridiculous.

I still remember a story; somebody had narrated to me when I was still a child. He told me about an old woman, who used to earn her livelihood by spinning yarn on her hand-driven spin-wheel from the rouleau of cotton-wool. Once she happened to see a cart loaded with cotton bales passing through her street. The moment she looked at the cart, she thought that she would have to spin all the cotton that was being carried over the cart and she started exclaiming, "For God's sake, how shall I be able to spin so much cotton?" Out of shock, she turned mad. Many people turn mad whenever some thing shocking occurs in their life. Their mental condition gets so much disturbed that they lose the balance of their mind. They start behaving like an insane person. This story should help such people to do not get unduly disturbed whenever some crisis may come in their life.

Had Kalidas committed a mistake in marrying Vidyuttama? Or had Vidyuttama committed a mistake? Both of them had committed a mistake. But Kalidas converted the mistake into a stepping stone for his success. If Kalidas could, we too can. Can't we?

Some people crumble but some people try to overcome the shocks like a hero. Many people commit such blunders at some occasions that they repent later on, through out their life. So it is better to keep in mind how different people react when they face a catastrophic situation. This way we can also keep our mind in balance irrespective of the type of calamity we may have to face.

Some people look out for someone who may console them or sympathize with them. But for some, shocks work like a scalpel of a neuro-surgeon. The shocks shake and modify the neural networks of their brains so much that they emerge as great geniuses. The rust over their neural circuits gets pealed off and what we see is a clean bright intellect that lied beneath the layers of rust. They come out in their new avatars as great scholars and intellectual icons. Shocking incidents come in their life as big opportunities as had happened in case of Kalidas.

5 Story of the Mother of Pandavas

Within the epic "Mahabharata", we get fine example of poor parenting. We can take a lesson from this epic which was pertinent not only during the days of Mahabharata, it has not lost its pertinence even today.

Sometimes the parents are so much worked up that they consider it a waste of time to listen to what their children want to tell them. Actually whatever may be the compulsions, we should first listen and then only tell them what they should do. Had Kunti, the mother of the Pandavas cared to listen to her children when they so eagerly wanted to tell her about the trophy they had won in the Swayamvara in which Arjun had won the hand of "Draupadi", the beautiful daughter of the king of Panchala, Drupad, through his extraordinary valour, not only she would have not told them to share the trophy perhaps even the Great War of Mahabharata would have not been fought. She had not imagined that the trophy they had won was an eminent princess.

At the time when Pandavas were living incognito in a village Ekachakra, disguised as *brahmins* instead of princes, they were asked by their Guru to go to see the *Swayamvara* of Draupadi in which she was going to select a suitor for her marriage. Her father wanted to make the most valorous man his son-in-law with whose help he might recapture the half of his kingdom that Arjuna had captured for Drona a few years back in a battle. So he had announced that Draupadi would select the prince or the king who could string a particular bow and hit a particular target that would be told in the *Swayamvara* itself as her suitor, using the same bow. The Pandavas also went to see the *Swayamvara* but had to sit amidst the general public. When no king or prince could even string the bow, the king opened the *Swayamvara* to the common people also. When the competition got opened for all, Arjuna still garbed as an ordinary *brahmin*, walked into the arena where he not only strung the bow, he also hit the target which he was told to hit to become eligible to marry Draupadi. The father of Draupadi, pleased with his feat, announced that he had won the hand of Draupadi, who despite being dark-complexioned, was reputed as the most beautiful princess.

Excited by the victory, when they came back with Draupadi to the camp where they were staying during the *Swayamvara*, they thought of breaking the news to their mother, Kunti. They said, "Look at the trophy we have won today, Mom." But Kunti did not care to listen or look at the trophy and told them to share the trophy among them. Obedient as they were, they decided to make Draupadi, their common consort. Draupadi also thought it might have been a part of her destiny only. So she also gave her consent. But Kauravas, the cousins of Pandavas, started teasing Pandavas. They even started talking in an insulting manner with Draupadi.

Had Kunti listened to her sons what his sons had won or what trophy they had brought with them, she would have never told them to share the trophy like this. She even tried to convince her sons that a woman could not be shared like this. But the Pandavas did not want her to change the decision she had already given.

Once after the marriage in a gambling game, Pandavas had put Draupadi at stake but lost her to Kauravas. They lost every thing they possessed. Having lost every thing, Pandavas proposed to Kauravas to give them just five villages where they could live and spend the rest of their life. But they refused to give even an inch of land to them, which eventually resulted in the Great War "Mahabharata".

Quite possibly this war would have not been fought if the Pandavas would not have had a common consort. Who could be blamed for such a colossal mistake? None else but Kunti. Don't you think so?

This story gives a useful tip that we, the parents should first listen to what the children want to tell us even if we may be short of time or preoccupied with some other thoughts before telling them what they should do.

Sometimes it may so happen that our child may be in a big enigma. But how can we know his problem unless we lend our ear to him and listen to him with patience? By keeping ourselves aloof from them we can push them sometimes into a big trouble for which we may have to repent for whole of our life later as you would find in the next story.

6 *Story of Karyl Chastain Beal*

I picked up this story from the book, "Chicken Soup for the Unsinkable Soul". This is a story Karyl Chastain Beal wrote to make the people aware of the importance of keeping themselves well knitted with their children so that they too may not commit the mistake she had committed.

She got so much aggrieved for not having looked deep into the psycho of her daughter. Had she been a little more vigilant probably her daughter Arlyn would have not committed suicide. But she never suspected that she could ever do so. Her only mistake was that she didn't know about the symptoms of a bipolar disorder. So she always carried an impression that her daughter was a girl who found joy in living. Karyl also thought that her daughter was in tune with Nature. But she was wrong. It was only after Arlyn committed suicide that she got a shock of her life from which she couldn't recover through whole of her life.

Quite confused about what should have caused her daughter to take such a step she collected all the bills her daughter had written in her own hand and found that some of them read as under.

"I keep asking myself why. For my entire life, all I have ever wanted was to be dead, to not be. Why?"

"I don't know why I didn't kill myself in fifth grade when I had the chance."

When Arlyn was in sixth grade, ten years old, her school had held a talent contest in which she had sung a song "Wind Beneath My Wings" which had been popularized those days by Bette Middler so well that she had been awarded a trophy for her performance. While driving back, Karyl had asked her, "When you sing, do you think about the words?" to which she had replied, "When I sing

'Wind Beneath My Wings,' I always think of you." So it never crossed her mind that this girl could ever think of taking such an extreme step. Totally confounded to understand after all what led her to take such a step, she and her husband turned her writings over to a psychiatrist for a "psychological autopsy" (an evaluation of someone based on information from their writings or other sources). It is only when the psychiatrist told them that Arlyn was suffering from bipolar disorder, that is, she was manic-depressive they could come to know what was wrong with her.

He apprised them that Arlyn knew that "something" was not right and due to this reason she used to remain tormented by confusion, shame and fear. He explained that the chemicals in her mind were imbalanced and that they had altered her perceptions of reality. This chemical imbalance had also produced her thoughts of suicide. The psychiatrist also told them that her brilliant mind made it possible for Arlyn to hide this part of herself from others. He insisted that she did not want to die.

It is only after what the psychiatrist told Karyl that she started reading about this disease. Had she read about it earlier, she would have saved her eighteen years old daughter from committing suicide. You can see how much shattered she should have been when she must have written, "If we really knew the future, we would alter our behaviour profoundly. Since we don't, however, we simply plod along; oblivious to the fact that disaster may happen at any moment. If I had known Arlyn's last day alive would have been August 7, 1996, I would have focussed on her exclusively. I would have quit my job to spend more time with her. I would have unplugged the telephone and television, so I could listen to her more carefully. I would not have let her out of my sight for even a nanosecond, so I could have savored her presence. Nothing else would have mattered. But I did not know. One of the most profound lessons Arlyn's death has taught me is that the only guaranteed moment is this one; therefore, if we live our lives expecting a future that may not exist, we may regret our choices forever."

Another lesson we can take from this story is what O.A. Battista wanted us to understand, that is, "The greatest weakness of most humans is their hesitancy to tell others how much they love them while they're alive."

When the children pass through teenage or adolescence, we often think it won't do them any harm if we upbraid them for their out-of-tune actions and forget what would happen if they might take an extreme step as Arlyn had taken. When we rebuke them or reprimand them, we forget how they may react if we keep on ignoring them or scolding them.

After getting this shock, she started disseminating the message that the parents should pay more personal attention to the behaviour of their children so that they do not remain in an illusion that everything is fine with them even when it may not be so.

By saying that we should think that this moment may be the last moment for us, it looks she only wanted to emphasize that if we love somebody we should not speak kind words in a very miserly way. May be, we may not get a chance to say the sort of words we keep in our heart but don't utter. We should not wait for a tomorrow for who knows a tomorrow may not come at all. At the end of the story she has written, "It only takes a little more effort to listen carefully, to give an extra hug, to say kind words. A moment given now may prevent a lifetime of regret" and has cited the following words of Harriet Beecher Stowe.

"The bitterest tears shed over graves are for the words left unsaid and deeds left undone."

Mrs Karyl's only mistake was that she didn't try to find out that her daughter was manic-depressive. Had she spent more time with her daughter her daughter would not have committed suicide because she would have come to know why she was unhappy. If she had spent more time with her daughter she would have been able to sense that her daughter had a disorder of this type. It is seen that when people who are manic-depressive say that they may finish their life, they mean it and may really end their life. So we shouldn't take that someone who may talk like this, is just wolfing.

Such persons need more love in their family than may be enough for a normal person. Non-medicos can commit a blunder as Karyl had committed because they are generally not fully aware of the possible consequences of not taking timely help of a psychiatrist in such cases.

So it is necessary that we understand how important is it to be in touch with the ethos of our children so that they may open their heart to us and tell us all about their feelings as they would tell any of their friends and may not feel neglected. When the parents spend enough time with their children they feel reassured that they are being looked after well. It gives them an assurance that their parents love them and would keep on looking after their needs and lend them an ear when they may like to convey what is perturbing them.

In the joint-family system, the grand parents and other elderly people of the family used to share the burden of looking after the children. But when the parents are all alone to look after them it may not be so easy for them to spend enough time with the children and give them enough attention. But they have to find out, how to do justice to the job and the children both.

7 Story on Existence of a Super Judicial System in The World

It is generally believed that whosoever created the Universe, also created a judicial system to ensure that the defaulters may get punished and the clear conscious people who get unduly punished may get rewarded. But because this system sometimes rewards or punishes the next of the kin instead of the persons who may have defaulted or got unduly punished, we often tend to lose faith in the existence of a system of this type.

This story restores our faith in the existence of a system that maintains law and order in the world, in its own way.

This incident takes me back to 1967 when I had just married. During those days I used to work at Bharat Heavy Electricals Limited, Tiruchirapalli in Tamilnadu. Though I was an engineer I had married a doctor. Luckily a few months after my marriage our company announced some vacancies in the company for the doctors. Our company had a hospital of its own for the treatment of the employees and their dependents within its campus.

The company had a policy of giving preference to the dependents of the employees to fill its vacancies. So I asked my wife to apply for the post against these vacancies. I was very hopeful that my wife would get selected because I was a North Indian and the Chief Medical Officer of the company was also a North Indian. There were very few persons from the North in the company at that time. Some were from Gujarat, some from Maharashtra, some from Punjab, some from Madhya Pradesh and Uttar Pradesh. Being very few in numbers we were all good friends among ourselves. Though the Chief Medical Officer was from Maharashtra, we had good relations with him also.

But we were surprised when after the interview of my wife I did not hear any word from the Chief Medical Officer. So I phoned up at his house and came to know that he had gone out of station for some official work and was expected to come back only after a week or so. His wife however gave us a hint that her husband had found some requirement not getting fulfilled in case of my wife. So her husband had not cleared the name of my wife for appointment.

Since my wife had been working in the Provincial Medical Services of Haryana prior to marriage and had earned very good reputation there, she rang up the General Manager of the company and told him about the objection the Chief Medical Officer had raised. She beseeched him for taking a lenient view of the objection because it could disrupt our marriage that was not even a year old yet.

The General Manager heard to the plea of my wife very compassionately and contacted some very senior doctor to take his opinion about the objection the Chief Medical Officer had raised. This doctor noted on the selection file that the objection raised by the Chief Medical Officer would not come in way of my wife's discharging the nature of duties she was going to perform. So the General Manager overruled the objection the Chief Medical Officer had raised and my wife got appointed as a doctor in the company.

But I got so angry with the behaviour of the Chief Medical Officer that I could not resist cursing him that he may go and work in a hospital of lepers.

While we forgot about this incident and resumed our relations, to our great surprise within three months of this incident, we came to know that the Chief Medical Officer had carried out an operation of Appendectomy on the wife of the General Manager which he came to know, was not at all required to be done. The General Manager got so angry with the Chief Medical Officer that he asked him to look for some job else where and leave the company within a month.

Though the doctor applied for a job at several places but he could not get a job anywhere. So he had to leave the company without a job in hand. He did not even tell us out of shame where he was planning to go. We however came to know after an year or so that he was working in a missionary Leprosy Hospital about sixty kilometers away from Tiruchirappalli. Though all of us went to felicitate him at his new place, I was surprised at the manner in which the curse I had given had materialized. I wondered whether there was really some eternal system that takes care of the wishes we make or the curses and the blessings we give to others.

I could not understand whether the Appendectomy operation he had carried out was only a matter of chance or was it merely a part of the plan of the eternal system which had decided to punish him for having cheated us a few months back in case of my wife. But the fact that he got a job in a leprosy hospital only has kept me guessing till today whether some system is in place that fulfills our wishes, curses and blessings.

Unless there is some system of this type the following sequence of events would perhaps have not taken place after I cursed him that he may have to work in some leprosy hospital.

(i) The Chief Medical Officer conducted an operation that was not necessary.

(ii) The General Manager got offended by this conduct of the Chief Medical Officer.

(iii) The General Manager asked him to submit his resignation.

(iv) The Chief Medical Officer could not find a job for several months after his resignation even though he was an FRCS.

(v) Finally he got a job in a leprosy hospital only.

This story corroborates the concept of *karma.* We of course are not able to understand how such a system should be working.

We are not able to understand how the curses and blessings should get materialized. But this story evinces that some system definitely exists. The reason why we should have faith in the existence of some system is that we shall commit fewer crimes in our life if we are conscious of the existence of a system of this type in the world. Though we may get exonerated by the courts of our land somehow, we should not expect that the eternal system would exonerate us.

8 Story of Shakya Muni

It is true that everybody has to die someday but when somebody dies when he is at the threshold of becoming the sole earning member of a family, such loss generally creates immense emotional stress in the family. We generally call such a death an untimely death.

No loss can be more heart rendering to a family than the loss of its sole earning member especially if all other members of the family may be either still minors or too old to earn for the family.

The compensation that a family may get may not be enough to let it stand on its own feet. So loss of a member of family is generally a loss that creates a lot of emotional stress in the family which may get bereaved.

Quite a number of people go into deep depression when they find that they have landed in a situation which has gone out of their control. A person who may have led a princely or princessly life earlier can go into such a state of mind if he or she may have to live as a dependent of somebody. When a woman may become a widow and her husband may not have left her enough money for her subsistence or she may have no place to go and spend the rest of her life at her own, she may go into a shock especially if she has also to settle her children in life yet.

However even under such situations, we should never think that no relief would ever come from any corner. We may have some hardships for a few years. But eventually we may find that we are able to put things in order somehow. Sometimes it may even so happen that if we cross the stage of these hardships, we may even occupy such a comfortable position of which we may not have even imagined ever.

Every happening is a part of our destiny. So we should never lose heart. Nor we should go into a pathological depression when some body may die. If there was a chance of saving a life through medical aid or surgical aid but the aid could not be provided for some reason beyond our control we should accept it as an act of destiny and try to bear the loss instead of losing heart. Though we can't feel happy when some body may die in our family, we should remain confident that some day, some solution would definitely emerge. We should try to come out of the grief and do some thing constructive about the circumstances that may arise.

Here is a story which can relieve us of our agony at such occasions.

It is said that once a woman had come to Shakya Muni when she lost her child, wailing at the top of her voice and she begged him to bring her baby back to life. Shakya Muni comforted her and offered to prepare a medicine that would revive her child. To make the medicine, he said, he would need a mustard seed, which he instructed her to find in a nearby village. But he told her that this mustard seed would have to come from a home that had never experienced the death of a family member. The woman set out from house to house, but nowhere could she find a home that had never known death. As she continued her quest, the woman began to realize her suffering was something shared by all the people. She was not alone to have had an experience of this type. Though every body knows that death is inevitable, people still wish that it should not occur in their family. So it needs an enlightenment of the type Shakya Muni had given to this woman.

The way we have adjusted our mind that the sun will rise in the east and set in the west, we have to also adjust our mind to the fact that some day every body has to die. It makes no sense to repent on something, which is as unchangeable as the directions in which the sun rises or sets or other natural events occur in the world.

We should also not think that somebody had an untimely death. Nothing in the world is untimely. God has made all systems so perfect that if all the things would have been not going in a timely manner, the world would have ceased to exist by now.

To have such an attitude, we have to see how everything in the realm of God, follows a perfect time-schedule. We can clearly see how every thing is so well timed. Take the case of the development of all the organs of the body in a foetus. Development of all the limbs as well as all internal organs such as liver, heart, kidneys and the brain follows a strictly well laid time schedule in a manner that the whole body of all creatures gets developed within their respective gestation periods. This shows how much attention God or the Creator of all the creatures has paid to the time-management. So we should believe that every thing that happens in our life has some strong basis and if something has a basis, we should never mind it. It is just like standing in a queue. If we come in time, we can get a chance earlier than others. Someday we may be at the back and some day, even at the front. So we should not mind whether we are at the back of the queue or in the front. Much same, is the case with the deaths. Some people die early, some people late.

Some natural calamities also keep on arising during our life. Take the case of the thousands of tourists who had gone to Thailand's beaches where in 2004, Tsunami waves had swept them away into the ocean. They had not committed any mistake. It would have been a mistake only if they would have been warned that Tsunami waves would hit the beaches and they would have ignored the warning. But that was not the case.

In such cases our destiny plays the upper hand and we commit a mistake under its influence. We don't have any control over the move the destiny makes in our life. It is not that our destiny always plays the upper hand. It lets us also play the upper hand. It lets us also plan our affairs the way we may like.

Just think of Kalpana Chawla and her co-astronauts who had all got burnt in the space shuttle by which they were returning after their space mission. They could have not saved themselves by not letting the outer layer of refractory tiles of the shuttle get ripped away. Nor the scientists at the Control Station could have saved them. So we have to believe in the role the destiny can play in our life also. Should we say, this tragedy had happened due to human neglect? The tragedy would have not occurred had the scientists checked the condition of the outer tiles before the shuttle was mounted on the rockets that had taken their space ship into the space. Even if they would have done so, the shuttle could have hit some debris floating in the space. So we can't say, the tragedy had happened only due to human negligence. This taught the scientists a lesson that they should be more cautious about such possibilities also in future.

Also think of the tragedy that had occurred in the chemical plant of Alfred Nobel in Norway. The entire plant had blown up into air. But his destiny later on took them to a place in Germany where they stumbled on kieselguhr which they could use as a packing medium for the safe transportation of the chemical they used to manufacture.

We die also only when our destiny wants us to die. The date and place of birth and the date and time of death, both are not in our own hands. We may live beyond hundred years and also live a short life due to no fault of ours. We can take precautions, no doubt. But our destiny saves us also many a times in our life when we come very close to death but the death looks the other way and we are saved. Just count such occasions and you would feel happy how miraculously you had escaped death at all such occasions.

9 *Role of Destiny in Alfred Nobel's Life*

We should remember the words of Robert Collier "All of us have bad luck and good luck. The man, who persists through the bad luck and keeps right on going, is the man who is there when the good luck comes and is ready to receive it." We always have some ups and downs in our life. We commit fewer mistakes when we pass through a lucky period of our life.

What can describe better than the discovery of Kieselguhr in the life of Alfred Nobel? Though he was able to develop the manufacturing process of Nitroglycerine, the chemical for which though there was lot of demand from several countries, he could have not succeeded to ship the chemical to these countries had he not been able to discover kieselguhr. It was his good luck that an incident led him to discover a type of soil which enabled him to safely transport this chemical to meet its demand.

Had he not been able to discover this unique type of soil he would have not been able to make so much money as he was able to. Nor would he have been able to make the type of Will he had made by virtue of which the Nobel Prizes are conferred every year for extraordinary contributions in the five fields he had specified in his Will. We should also therefore not feel despondent if we face some serious problems in our life. If we have good destiny we too can hope that our destiny may lend a helping hand to us at such occasions as it had done in case of Alfred Nobel.

Here is the story of the incident that had led him to this discovery.

Though he and his son had been able to evolve the method of manufacturing Nitroglycerine, they did not have a method of packing it for transportation so that it did not explode in transit. Though many countries were interested to purchase this chemical from them, they were afraid to place an order on them because it was extremely dangerous to handle it at the shipyards and warehouses. It was not safe to be stored even in their own warehouses. Once their entire plant in Norway, had blown up into sky. Just a few weeks later, in Silesia, when a worker was trying to cut the frozen blasting oil with an axe at a site, his legs had blown off more than half a mile away. Once all the seventy cans filled with the explosive that were being transported by a ship, had blown up aboard the ship docked in Panama which had wrecked even the wharf and a nearby warehouse.

So they were desperately looking for some method of safe packing for the transportation of this explosive.

We can call it simply a matter of luck that one day, somewhere in north Germany, when some porters while towing a few cans of this explosive found one of the cans leaking. First they looked for sawdust to soak the oil that had spread on the floor. But when they couldn't lay hands on sawdust, they tried to put kieselgühr, an earth found in that area. Alfred Nobel was amazed at the way the earth drank up the oil just like a blotting paper. Immediately it struck to him that kieselgühr could be used to transport the explosive without any risk. This solved their problem. They started making putty by mixing three parts of the oil with one part of kieselgühr, for transporting the explosive.

Soon he was flooded with orders. After that, what happened is known all over the world. Within ten years, his fifteen plants started turning out six million pounds of the explosive to meet the demand for the explosive from various countries.

He made so much money that he thought of putting it to some proper use. In his Will, he made a provision of distributing the five awards known as Nobel Prizes every year from the interest accrued on the deposits he made in a bank of Sweden for this purpose. It looks providence wanted him to institute the Nobel Prizes. Had his team not been able to discover kieselgühr, perhaps, you can guess what would have happened!

But it all happened because he did not stop manufacturing the explosive even after the incident of explosion at his Norwegian plant and subsequent explosions that took place during the transportation of the chemical. He never gave up the hope that someday he would be able to find some safe way of transporting the explosive. Just think, what would have happened had Alfred Nobel given up manufacturing in his plants. Or had the explosive not leaked at a place where the soil contained kieselgühr. But it looks the Nature let the leakage occur at the place where it had exactly leaked that day.

We may categorize various types of problems we may face in our life into following categories.

(i) The problems we can solve all by ourselves.

(ii) The problems we can not solve without taking help of others.

(iii) The problems for which we also need intervention of the celestial energy.

The problem Alfred Nobel was facing was of the third type. Though one can not be sure whether the celestial energy would come to one's rescue, we can still wait and hope that such a help may come forth. If we don't give up our efforts the chances are Nature may help us also in our life.

10 Story of Shalik Yadav

This incident relates to Shalik Yadav, who had a grocery shop in the Nilmatha Ibrahimpur locality of the Cantonment area of Lucknow.

On the evening of July 22, 2006 when he was busy attending to his customers all of sudden his attention drew toward a girl approaching his shop, who was being chased away by a young man. He saw that the youth had caught hold of the girl before she could reach the shop. When the girl tried to wriggle out the youth pushed her down. Suspecting the youth to have criminal antecedents, none except Shalik Yadav of the onlookers mustered courage to oppose his indecent act. Unable to bear this act he left the shop to help the girl and brought her to the shop. He even identified the youth and warned him that he would hand him over to the police if he ever indulged in such acts.

Though the youth left the scene after this incident he nonetheless threatened him of dire consequences before leaving the place.

Shalik informed the Cantonment-police about the incident hoping that it would intervene and punish the youth for his misdoing. But the police sent merely two constables to look into the matter. Neither the Station House Officer nor the Beat In-charge deemed it fit to visit the place and resolve the issue. After two days at about 9 p.m., about a dozen youths led by the youth, whom Shalik had admonished, arrived at his shop and started beating up him brutally even as two constables, as mentioned in the local newspapers, were also present nearby. Hearing screams, locals rushed for his rescue and both the groups resorted to brick batting. While the groups were engaged in a pitched battle, a few of youths from the errant youth's group pounced upon Shalik and hit him with bricks on his head leaving him unconscious. While the assailants fled the scene, the victim was rushed to the Medical

University's Trauma Centre. However, he succumbed to the head injuries the next day in the early hours of 25th July. The cops later arrested the father of the youth. But now there was no one to look after Shalik's parents and his two small children because he was the lone breadwinner of the family.

What you would have done in this case? Don't you think Shalik was at fault? In India, police does not help a common man most of the time. So if you are only a common man, you should not hope that police would come in time to help you when you are in some trouble. It was the fault of Shalik that he counted too heavily on the police. Had the police responded to Shalik's complaint soon after the incident of 22nd July, he would not have been beaten to death on 24th July and have had such an end. This incident tells us that if you are the sole earning member of your family, you shouldn't get so much involved in an incident directly as Shalik got involved. Even if he got involved out of humanitarian reasons he should have not warned the young man of dire consequences because he had no means of self-protection other than the police. One has to weigh what is more important for him in life — to take care of own family or to set right the erring people. There is nothing wrong in setting right the erring people but it should be done in a manner that one's family does not suffer in the process.

11 *Story of Avinash Mahajan who Got Slaughtered in his Factory*

I still shudder with awe whenever I recall the ghastly incident of the murder of one of my colleague, Avinash Mahajan in 1991. He was the Works Manager of the "Die Casting Shop" of Scooters India Limited, Lucknow.

It was around 9 a.m. when we got the news that a workman of Avinash Mahajan had struck him with his knife on his legs and he kept on attacking him till he fell down on the floor dead. He had cut him into several pieces. He had made this knife in the factory itself with the sole intention of killing him only.

The news spread like wild fire. Everybody wondered what had offended this worker so much. When we inquired about the reason we came to know that just a few days back Avinash had chastised this worker that he should not absent himself from his workplace without taking prior permission of his supervisor. He had also told him that he didn't pay proper attention to his work. But when the worker did not pay heed to his instructions he once again told him to behave in a disciplined manner. But the worker felt so much offended at his telling him to work as a disciplined worker that he prepared a butcher's knife in the factory and hid it in his cupboard to kill Mahajan if he ever reprimanded him again. We came to know that this man used to abscond from work for several hours almost every day without informing his supervisor.

As the witnesses told, Mahajan told this workman once again to mend his ways or he would take disciplinary action against him. The worker got so much enraged when he was told to behave in a disciplined manner that he hit him with the knife first on his legs and then on other parts of his body till he became lifeless.

We later on came to know that this worker belonged to a butcher-family. His father had a mutton shop in a village close to the factory and he only used to butcher the goats for the meat sold in the shop.

No doubt a manager has to discipline his workmen but was Mahajan not expected to know what type of man this workman was? Had he known that this worker belonged to a butcher family, perhaps he would have acted more cautiously.

12 *Story of the Young Executive Manjunath*

When we are young the people who have been taught to lead an ethical life at home, are generally not able to tolerate that some body may sell adulterated goods to people without their knowledge that they have been sold adulterated goods. Whether we call it an overdose of ethics at home or lack of judgment what is more important in life, it is sad that many people lose their life in the battle of ethics and personal survival.

Here is the story of Manjunath Shanmugam, who had done his MBA from IIM, Lucknow and was working as a Marketing Executive in Indian Oil Corporation. He was in-charge of the eastern territory of Uttar Pradesh. On 19th November 2005 he had been murdered by the henchmen of an Oil Mafia, who had a Petrol Pump in Lakhimpur Kheri District of Uttar Pradesh because Manjunath wanted to cancel his license of petrol pump as he kept on selling adulterated petrol despite of having been served several warnings.

Manjunath did not have any body else in his family to support the family. Still he preferred to teach this dealer a lesson without suspecting that he was risking his life by doing so. After his death the dreams of his parents came to an end. They thought, the employers of their son would help them. But don't you think, whatever the company in which he worked might have done for them, it could never replace the loss they had incurred? But Manjunath did not think of it despite being so well qualified.

It may be enough if we are ourselves ethical. We should think of making others also as ethical as we may be, only if we are not concerned with how our family would live if someone kills us. If we may be the main earning member of our family we should not attempt to be a reformer. We have to keep in mind, while it is good to be righteous, we have to teach a lesson in a manner that though we may kill a snake, the stick we use to kill it should not get broken in the process. We should think what would be the fate of our family if we lose our life. We should select a course that may serve both purposes, that is, which may teach the other person a lesson and we may also not lose our life. If we leave our family unprotected after sacrificing our life the chances are, our family and siblings or the children would only abhor us after our death for having laid down our life in such a manner. Only in rare circumstances they may appreciate or praise us for having stuck to righteousness even at the cost of our life. They may even discard righteousness in their life. To lay life for the nation is quite a different thing but to teach a lesson to an individual without bothering about the safety of our family can't be considered much sensible.

If we also lay our life like Shalik or Manjunath, no one would suffer so much in life as our own family and our children. So much emphasis on righteousness may have only a negative effect on their personality. Instead of following the path of righteousness, our children may follow the path of unrighteousness because they had to pass a life amidst misfortunes because of the righteousness of their parents. So we should know how much ideological we can afford to be. Though the courts finally passed a punishment of life imprisonment to the main offender of the murder in 2009, how would it help his family?

To learn something from the above situations may appear to be silly at the first instance because of the logic that many of such situations may not occur in our life. But if we think so we should think the same way about what we learn from our own experiences too. It is far easier to learn from the mistakes of others than from only our own mistakes.

13 *Stories of the Mothers of Thomas Alva Edison and Albert Einstein*

Same school. Same college. Just think, how is it that some of the students of the same school and same college become big inventors, big scientists, big industrialists or big politicians. But the rest of them are not able to attain any significant status in their lives. What are the factors that make some of the students, big names but every one does not make a mark in the world?

We can say, the parents make the difference. We ourselves also make the difference. If you don't believe, these stories would change your mind. If Albert Einstein could become what he had become in his life, it was all due to his parents. Had his parents not cared, he would have been removed from the school where he used to study. Much same was the case of the great inventor, Thomas Alva Edison also. So the parents have to bear in mind the role they can play in the lives of their children. What the children become in life depends to a great extent, though it is not always so, much on the efforts their parents make to build them.

The parents should not feel disheartened if the school of their children may inform them that their children are not performing well in the school as long as they follow the examples of the parents of Albert Einstein and Thomas Alva Edison.

Here are their stories which tell, why.

The schools compare the performance of a child according to their own criteria. But they often fail to identify the students who are far more talented than any one might be able to think during their school days.

Let's take the case of Thomas Alva Edison. He was born in 1947 in Ohio, US of America, in a family of Dutch origin. He had to quit school after three months when he was ridiculed for his wandering mind. We know Edison for the inventions he had made. So what made the difference? His mother made all the difference who was a school teacher in Canada. After he quit the school, she took over the responsibility of his education. She lovingly encouraged him to read and experiment. This attitude of hers filled his mind with a zeal to do something that must not disappoint her as was obvious from what he had said of her, "My mother was the making of me. She was so true, so sure of me; and I felt had something to look for, someone I must not disappoint." It is this type of thinking his mother had planted in his mind that gave him the strength to remain firm irrespective of any adversities in life.

As is well known he had not only invented the incandescent lamp, he actually had 1097 US patents to his name besides many in UK, France and Germany. It is well known that he didn't flinch even when his efforts to produce an incandescent bulb, which would light up by electricity failed for almost 10,000 times. We have to take a lesson from him.

This is what he said of his failures, "I have not failed. I've just found 10,000 ways that won't work." Credit goes to the type of training his mother gave him during his childhood. She didn't ridicule or discourage him, when he was turned out of his school. We should also have the same spirit for our children.

Pauline Einstein, the mother of Albert Einstein had also demonstrated great patience just like the mother of Thomas Alva Edison. It may not be known to many but the fact is that Albert Einstein had spoken his first words as late as at the age of four. But his mother kept on getting him treated patiently and compassionately through out his childhood. Even when in school, his class teacher had sent the complaint that he was not able to solve even simple problems of mathematics. Little did the teacher know that one day the same boy would be considered as one of the best mathematicians of the world and the one to author the "Theory of Relativity". All parents take pains to help their children. All of us are what we are only because of the efforts our parents had taken during our school days and after the school days. Whatever efforts we make later on, we could have not made had they not taken care of our needs during the early days of our life.

To a great deal, we rise in our life due to the contributions and sacrifices our respective parents make during our childhood, only. During school days we don't have the capability to judge what is happening in our life and what could be the consequences of what may be happening in our life. Only the parents know what role they should play to ensure that we do not suffer in our life due to inadequate supervision or guidance.

14 *Story of Wilma Rudolf's Parents*

While all parents want to take the best care of their children, sometimes they are so hard pressed by their job commitments that it becomes difficult for them to find sufficient time for them. The children in such cases feel neglected and they even start doubting whether they really love them or only feign to love them.

The doctors, for instance, have to attend to their patients even if some one may turn up exactly when they may have taken their bag to go home. If they have to attend to a patient, they forget what awaits them at home. They immediately give priority to the patient because they know it is more urgent for them to save the life of the patient. They give more attention to the patients than any thing else. For them every other work assumes secondary importance. But their children have to bear the brunt of the nature of their work that makes them pay more attention to the patients. Their children wait at home when their parents are looking after some patient at their clinic or nursing home or in the hospital where they may be engaged. Their children, obviously, pass through enormous emotional stress. Some children are able to cope up well but many find it difficult to cope.

This is the story of the parents of Wilma Rudolf. This story shows how some parents help their children to fulfill their dreams that may appear to be almost impossible. They don't let their children have a feeling that they have some handicap even if they have a handicap. They help them to overcome their handicaps. We can get inspiration from such cases.

What difference the parents can make, can be understood when we look at the role the parents of Wilma Rudolf had played. Wilma had been honoured as the "Athlete of the Year" in 1960 by the

US of America despite the fact that at the age of 12, she used to wear a leg brace. She had been struck with polio at the age of 12 and all the doctors had told her parents that she wouldn't even be able to walk. But her family helped her diligently with the help of different type of oil massages, so that she was not only able to walk again, she even started taking part in the races again. Everybody got surprised when they saw her not simply participate in the races but they saw that she could set a world record for the 200-meter dash when in the university and later even won three Olympic medals for United States, in the track events.

Wilma had attributed her success to the efforts taken by her parents and said that all the credit for these medals should actually go to them instead of her.

This is the type of dedication all the parents need to have towards the welfare of their children.

Though how much indebted we may feel to our parents depends on how well they had looked after us, yet if we don't feel indebted to them at all it is a mistake on our part. By giving birth to us they give us an opportunity to make our destiny ourselves. They can't help us for whole of our life even otherwise. Parents always do what they can — good or bad. We have to build our destiny from the point where they may leave us in the world. We should not blame them any way.

There are many people who even lose their parents at quite an early age. Many of such people have been able to lead quite an exemplary life. So we should never blame the parents even if we may feel, they did not look after us properly.

15 *Kathy Johnson Gale's Story "Blameless"*

Many of us reason out why we should not condemn our parents even if they did not look after us well during our childhood. This story tells why we should not blame them. There are parents who do not blame their children even if they may commit some blunder. In such cases don't you think the children should also reciprocate the same gesture to them?

Kathy Johnson Gale has told in this story, which was published in the book, "Chicken Soup for the College Soul" that in her own family her parents used to always point out on the dining table who was at fault whenever any body made a mistake. So she was highly impressed when she found that in the family of one of her friends, Jane White, nobody blamed anyone in the family even when any of them committed some serious mistake.

Whatever the children watch at home gets deeply imprinted in their subconscious mind. They actually do not sift the information that enters their mind into right and wrong. So whatever their parents tell them gets permanently planted in their mind. Even the attitudes of the parents get permanently planted in their minds. So the parents should restrain themselves much more while taunting or ridiculing the children than the adults. When we criticize or ridicule a child, it has a far more harmful effect on him or her than it may harm an adult. But there are both types of parents: those who don't criticize or ridicule their children as well as the ones who don't spare their children from being ridiculed.

This story can encourage anyone to give up the habit of criticizing the children if he or she may be in habit of criticizing the children whenever they commit a mistake. She found that the parents of Jane White did not place the blame on any one in the family, even under severe circumstances. She has narrated the incident in which Jane got killed.

She tells in this story an incident that when Sarah, her elder sister purchased a new car she planned to make a trip in her car along with her younger sisters Jane and Amy along with Kathy from their home in Florida to New York. On the way, Amy, the youngest one, who had just got her driving license, pressed Sarah to allow her to drive the car. So after having come out of the crowded area Sarah let Amy drive the car. But Amy didn't notice a stop sign at an intersection and continued into the intersection without stopping. Unluckily a driver of a large semi-tractor-trailer who was coming from the front side couldn't apply brakes in time and his vehicle ploughed into Sarah's car. While Kathy survived with only some bruises, Jane died instantly. Though Sarah and Amy also survived, Sarah had received a head injury and Amy's leg got fractured.

Kathy tells that she was surprised when Mr. and Mrs. White arrived at the hospital but didn't accuse or blame any one. To both of their daughters, and especially to Amy, over and over they simply said, "We're so glad that you are alive."

Later, when Kathy asked the Whites why they never talked about the fact that Amy should have not pressed to drive the car or have run a stop sign, Mrs. White said, "Jane's gone, and we miss her terribly. Nothing we say or do will bring her back. But Amy has her whole life ahead of her. How can she lead a full and happy life if she feels we blame her for her sister's death?"

This is the type of attitude we should also have as parents. If we may taunt a child for one activity, we should also praise him or her for the activity in which he or she may be superior. Also when the parents start comparing the children, it disturbs the mind of the child who is condemned. It never helps to condemn anyone, especially the children.

The children, who live under a hostile atmosphere at home, do not develop right habits. So the parents should not pass on their tensions to the children by beating them or by scolding them. Nor should they chide them, "What! You don't even know how to hold a knife and a fork properly", if they have not been taught how to hold a knife or a fork. If they are scolded when they eat food, they may even develop an aversion for the food. For the same reason the parents should also not chide the children for not dressing up in the manner they may have been told by them unless they have been also told the reason of not dressing up in the manner they dress up.

It is wrong to expect that somebody else would teach the children right attitudes. Nobody can teach them right attitudes better than the parents themselves.

For the children there can be no better school for learning right attitudes than the home itself. The parents have to provide right atmosphere at home so that they may learn things like how to help each other and how to resolve the conflicts peacefully without creating furor in the house. If the parents resolve their own conflicts in a peaceful manner the children would also learn the art of resolving their conflicts in the same manner.

It is not that the parents need not teach the children about the table manners or the dressing etiquette. What is being emphasized here is that it is more beneficial in life to have right attitudes and right outlook than to learn how to hold the fork and knife or how to dress up. It is not enough to learn only right manners. It is more important to develop right attitudes like not blaming the members of the family or to resolve all conflicts in a peaceful manner only.

16 *Jack Griffin's Story "It's Ok My Son. Everybody Does it"*

It is surprising that many parents want to follow some other pattern of attitudes for themselves than the pattern they want their children to follow. This is not the right way of teaching the children the type of attitudes they should have. This story of Jack Griffin sent a strong message to the parents for not adopting double standards of attitudes: one for themselves and another for the children. This is not the way they can teach the children how to get work done through fair means.

This story tells why the parents should not impress upon the mind of the children that there is no harm in getting our work in an illegal manner or through unfair means only.

This story had originally appeared in the Chicago Sun-Times in 1940's. It had later on appeared in the House Journals of several schools. It tells us why the parents should not allow their children to adopt unfair means for every thing, in life. Later on it was translated in several languages and published in many countries across the world.

Though situations do arise when one has to become unethical to a certain extent to make headway or to get going amidst the people who are unethical, it does not justify the use of unfair means all the time. It is for the parents to decide what they want to teach them. Actually we should set an example ourselves to demonstrate how to deal with the corrupt people in life successfully.

The main character of the story is Johnny, who was always made to observe how it helps one to get his work done by paying tips or bribes. Towards the end, the story tells what fate such people can expect eventually.

If you have already read this story you may skip it. Otherwise, you may read it now. It is reproduced verbatim, below:

"When Johnny was 6 years old, he was with his father when they were caught speeding. His father handed the officer a twenty-dollar bill with his driver's license. "It's OK, son", his father said as they drove off, "Everybody does it".

"When he was 8, he was present at a family council presided over by Uncle George, on the surest means to save points off the income tax return, "It's OK, kid.", his uncle said, "Everybody does it".

"When he was 9, his mother took him to his first theatre production. The box office man couldn't find any seats until his mother discovered an extra $5 in her purse. "It's OK, son", she said, "Everybody does it".

"When he was 12, he broke his glasses on the way to school. His Aunt Francine persuaded the insurance company that they had been stolen and they collected $75. "It's OK, kid," she said, "Everybody does it".

"When he was 15, he made right guard on the high school football team. His coach showed him how to block and at the same time grab the opposing end by the shirt so the official couldn't see it. "It's OK, kid," the coach said, "Everybody does it".

"When he was 16, he took his first summer job at the super market. His assignment was to put the overripe strawberries in the bottom of the boxes and the good ones on top where they would show. "It's OK, kid," the manager said, "Everybody does it."

"When he was 18, Johnny and a neighbour applied for a college scholarship. Johnny was a marginal student. His neighbour was in the upper 3 percent of his class, but couldn't play right guard. Johnny got the scholarship. "It's OK, son," his parents said, "Everybody does it."

"When he was 19, he was approached by an upper-class man, who offered the test answers for $50. "It's OK Kid," he said, "Everybody does it." Johnny was caught and sent home in disgrace.

"How could you do this to your mother and me?" his father said. "You never learned anything like this at home." His aunt and uncle were also shocked."

If there's one thing the adult world can't stand, it's a kid who cheats. The story tells, "Unless the parents set an example of neither accepting bribes nor offering bribes, their children may also end up with a similar fate as Johnny. So what the parents tell their children by way of setting an example plays a stronger role in shaping their personality and character."

Actually all parents should narrate this story to their children, so that they may at least know, the value of doing the things in a fair way. There are so many people who don't accept any gratification themselves but do not mind giving gratification to others because they know their work will get held up otherwise. Actually no hard and fast rules can be set about the use of ethical means. One has to weigh himself when to use the fair means and when the unfair means.

When to be ethical and when unethical, is a matter of one's own judgement. We should however use foul means only if that may be the only way to achieve our goal.

This story may not appeal to the people who earn money only by doling out favours to the people in power or who exploit the powers vested in them by the Government or by the constitutional body of the organization where they may be working. But it leaves a strong impact on the mind anyway.

It is said the character of a man gets revealed only when he has the scope of adopting unfair means but manages to get ahead in life without adopting unfair means.

17 *Story of the Principal of a Missionary School of Odisha (Orissa)*

When we are born we don't know to which school our parents would send us for studies. We don't know what type of school it would be. Nor do we know who will be the teachers or the principal of the school. Generally the parents decide the school where they can send us, according to their financial status and the transport arrangements they can afford.

The school where we study, however, as we know plays an important role in our life. The schools don't just impart education they also shape our general confidence in life. The parents usually go by the reputation of the school at the time of admitting us in it. They also keep in mind its distance from the residence so that it may not be inconvenient to send us to the school and also to collect us from there. But they can't foresee any untoward thing that may happen to us in the school after we have joined the school.

Here is a story that tells us what type of ordeal some children face sometimes. The principal may change or the management of school may change. Even sometimes the class teacher may not be of affectionate type.

So even though the parents may have taken a decision in the right earnest they can't be sure of certain things that may happen in the school. Parents generally think it is safe to send their children to a public school or a missionary school. But such instances belie even public's such confidence in the missionary schools.

Though all students are not harassed in a school, recently there have been several cases of harassment and ill treatment of the students of even Nursery and Prep Level in the schools. In some cases some children have been made to stand up in hot sun for hours and some children have been even asked to strip themselves and stand on their chairs in the class in front of their classmates. Teachers don't even think how humiliating it would be for the students. The whole pleasure of the students to whom such treatment may be meted may get lost. As such children find it traumatic to stay away from the parents in the school initially. Over this if they are not treated lovingly in the school, it becomes still more traumatic for them.

Children are generally punished in this manner if they have not completed their homework or have not paid the fees in time. In some schools of the girls, the male teachers and staff have been reported to have even sexually molested and abused the students. In some cases some teachers have been reported to have even beaten the children mercilessly to the extent for very minor faults of theirs that the children had to be rushed to a hospital for their treatment. Some teachers in some schools have been reported to have even slapped some children so hard that they had become deaf for ever. But the parents come to know of any such treatment having been given to their children only after they have already gone through some experience of this nature.

Here is a peculiar type of case that had appeared in the press in 2009 about a missionary school of Odisha. According to the reports published in the media, the principal of this school had started giving electric shocks to some students with an idea that the shocks so given would improve their performance in studies. The case that was highlighted the most was of a ten years old girl who had been subjected to this weird experiment by the principal of the school. The matter came to light when the child told about it to her mother. She had not told anyone about this type of treatment earlier thinking that it may be a normal practice. But when she showed the burn-marks to her mother, the mother got suspicious of something foul going on in the school.

Students are generally not able raise their voice against any thing of this type that may happen in their schools even if they may feel; it is not a correct thing. A child of such a small age even otherwise is not expected to judge why she is being given electric shocks. It was only when her mother asked her about the scars, she noticed on her legs and hands that she learnt about the travail of her daughter when she told that the principal had given her electric shocks to improve her proficiency. How unfortunate the girl was that she had to study in a school where she had to get such shocks just because it had an idiosyncratic principal. The mother gathered courage to report the matter to the police and it is learnt that though the principal tried to go underground, the police had succeeded to nab him.

Obviously the father of the girl had not committed any mistake because he could have not known that such a thing was likely to happen in the school.

Yet a question arises why such a thing had to happen in the life of this particular girl or her other school mates at all.

We can of course say that every event in our life happens only due to confluence of some situations. Some situations may arise due to our own mistakes but some situations can arise for no fault of ours also. If we think about the situations that had led to this occurrence we can list following factors.

(i) That the house of the girl happened to be close to this school.

(ii) That the parents of the girl got her admitted in this particular school because it was a missionary school.

(iii) That this school had a principal who got the idea of improving the performance of some students by giving them electric shocks.

(iv) That the principal thought he could carry out this experiment on this girl because her parents may not raise any objection, being of a poor class.

(v) That the principal did not take prior consent of the parents before subjecting their daughter to such a torturous process.

(vi) That the principal thought he could give the electric shocks himself and it was not necessary to consult or engage a psychiatrist for this job.

How many things had gone together for such a thing to have happened? It could also be perhaps thought to be a result of the *karma* of the girl's past life? While one can have the genes of his or her parents biologically how the karma of someone's past life can enter the mental system of somebody is a mere speculation of the past sages because it is unbelievable that any information about karma may ever remain intact unless it is recorded on some physical media. So much information can not be kept stored just in "vacuum" so that it may get transferred at a later date into a newborn's system.

Or may be the principal had seen some doctor giving electric shocks sometime during his childhood which had left some scar on his memory.

We don't know what actually had prompted the principal to carry out such an experiment. But that it was not justified to have subjected the girls to such an ordeal cannot be denied.

No one expects that such a thing can happen in a missionary school. But not just this type of thing, there are many things which surprise us in life. It is for this reason only why man keeps on praying that no such event may occur in his life or in his family.

Some people pray to God and some people go to the church or temple and pray that they may have enough strength to withstand any crisis through which they may have to pass in their life. The prayer gives them energy to face the crucial events of life more courageously.

We feel that there is a hand of God who has built this universe so flawlessly that it has survived so many trillions of years shielding us because we have prayed to Him. This thought itself gives us enough mental strength. We don't know whether God would protect us or not but what do we lose by praying? We can make all the preparations but some stray incident can still occur that may tilt the scales against us. It is seen that people who pray feel less distressed in life because when they pray positive vibrations surround them. So we should also pray to God that the events of the type that had happened in the life of this girl may not happen in our family.

18 *Story of an Examiner who used to Play with the Destinies of the Students*

Here is a story that tells how people sometimes become indiscriminate even when they do not intend to be indiscriminate. The circumstances make them indiscriminate. The story tells how such instances can affect the careers of a score of innocent people for no fault of theirs.

It is not uncommon to note that even the students who show an upbeat performance in the class rooms sometimes do not perform well in the examinations and those who had been laggards through out in the class rooms perform extremely well in the examinations. This story tells how the performances get juggled in the examinations. The poor performers sometimes get excellent marks in the examinations and the excellent students just get pass marks only. Such results often bewilder not only the students but their parents and teachers also.

But who suffer due to such incidents: the bright students? Obviously, the bright students who may have performed well but may not get as good marks as they deserve.

The elder brother of one of my close friends when I was a student of High School was a professor of geography in our college. Every year he used to get the answer-books of the Intermediate students from UP Higher Secondary Education Board for evaluation for awarding marks based on the performance of the students. But he always used to tell us that it was not at all possible for any one to examine so many books within the time the Board gave them for this purpose. So he had evolved a via media.

He used to fill the Summary Sheets of the marks secured by the students without even opening the bundles of the answer-books and dispatch the Summary-Sheets to the Board within prescribed time without evaluating the answer-books.

The Board had allowed him and as a matter of fact all the examiners like him, that they could evaluate the answer-books and send the Summary Sheets of the marks scored by the students to the Board first and dispatch the checked answer-books of the students afterwards at leisure.

Only after sending the Summary Sheets, he used to open most of the bundles of the examination-copies for evaluation. I often found him wailing that he had awarded too few marks to a student who had performed extremely well and very high marks to the students who had not at all deserved good marks. But during this process I noticed that he used to award the marks in the answer-books in a manner that the total of the marks awarded for individual questions tallied with the marks he had already filled in the Summary Sheets.

The marks secured in the Intermediate Examination in India play an important role in the students' further career. Whenever I recall the manner in which the professor used to check the answer-books I shudder with the thought, how time constraints sometimes can make men so unscrupulous.

Students do not know that their answer-books could be examined in such a casual manner. Even if they ask for re-evaluation of the answer-books, the Board arranges only to get whether there was some mistake in the totaling of the marks checked. But the professor always ensured that there was no totaling mistake.

Whatever may have been the constraints of the professor what surprises is his total indifference to the injustice he was doing to the students. The students who did not deserve good marks were getting high marks while the students who deserved to get high marks were getting poor marks. So he was obviously indulging in an unethical practice.

Should he have been playing a game with the destinies of the students like this? Just imagine how the students who have studied very hard through out the year to get good marks would feel when they find that they got marks much below their expectations. How difficult they would find to explain to their parents why they secured so poor marks in the examinations? Not suspecting what had actually happened they sometimes even commit suicide.

Should we say, it was not the fault of the professor alone? The Board was also responsible. The Board should have realized that it should have not sent so many answer-books to the same examiners if the time given to them was too short. It should have appointed more examiners instead of burdening the same examiners with so many answer-books.

What lesson we can take from this story? The lesson is clear. We should not play with the destinies of others under such circumstances.

19 *Story of a Brahmin who could not Annoy Lord Buddha by Abusing Him*

Different people act in a different way when they get annoyed and are not in a position to take any retaliatory action against the person who may have annoyed them. While some people decide to take a revenge later on when they may be in a position to take revenge, some people remain calm even when somebody tries his or her best to annoy them. They do not lose their temperament.

Of course it is not easy to excuse a defaulter but there are occasions when we should overlook the faults of others. We should only not let the other person think that we have not overlooked because we are not able to teach a lesson. If we excuse somebody due to weakness it does not serve any purpose. But if we excuse someone when he or she knows we could have punished him or her it can create a better relationship.

Here is a story that tells how we may control our temperament when somebody may go on pestering us unnecessarily.

This story is about a brahmin who wanted to prove to the world that Lord Buddha was also an ordinary man just like anyone else. The disciples of Lord Buddha laughed at him. So the brahmin thought of a way to prove his point. He thought that Lord Buddha would get annoyed if he continuously kept on abusing him just like any body else. To prove his point, he went to Lord Buddha and started abusing him. But when Buddha did not respond, he thought that Buddha had not probably heard them. So he went a little closer and started abusing him again. But to his great surprise even this did not make any difference. He noticed no change in Buddha's expression. Buddha did not lose his temper at all. So the brahmin started abusing him even more fiercely. However this too did not affect Buddha. He still showed the same serene smile on his face full of compassion as if nobody had abused him at all.

Tired, the brahmin asked him, "I have been abusing you since long but I am surprised why you did not get offended."

When he asked Buddha this question, Buddha said, "Dear brother, I did not get offended because I did not accept a single abuse from you." Surprised by what Buddha told him the Brahmin asked him, "But you would have heard the abuses anyway. Didn't you?"

Do you know what Buddha told him? He told him, "I didn't need any of those abuses. So why should I have even heard them?"

Puzzled, the brahmin asked, "What do you mean?" Buddha smiled and told him, "All those abuses remain with you." The brahmin couldn't quite get it. So he went on saying, "How is it possible? I have been constantly abusing you."

Buddha told him, "Yes, my friend. But I did not accept even a single abuse from you!" Even more puzzled, when the brahmin again asked, "What do you mean by not accepting the abuses?" Buddha told him, "Dear brother! Suppose, you give some coins to someone, but the other person does not accept them, with whom those coins will remain?"

The brahmin said, "The coins will obviously remain with me." Thereupon Buddha said, "You are right. The same has happened with your abuses. You came here and hurled abuses at me, but I did not accept a single abuse from you. Therefore all those abuses also remained with you only. Now you should have understood why I did not get angry with you?" The brahmin agreed that if a person refuses to accept somebody's abuses such abuses remain with the person who hurls the abuses, not the person on whom the abuses were hurled. Having understood this, the brahmin felt ashamed of having hurled abuses on Lord Buddha and he decided to become his disciple.

This story tells us, if we can have the same attitude as Lord Buddha had we, too, can keep ourselves cool even if somebody may point out our faults or may criticize or abuse us.

If we may introspect, we would find that bad temperament is a potential reason of committing mistakes. Due to bad temperament we sometimes commit such mistakes that we are not able to retrieve from the damage caused to us. We can save ourselves from committing several mistakes simply by training ourselves in a manner that we don't lose our temperament when we are abused by some one.

20 Story on Importance of Learning Good Manners in Life

This story tells why it is more important to learn good manners than just getting high academic or professional qualifications. Some highly qualified people also fail in life because they don't know how to behave at the workplace. Unfortunately in the colleges it is not customary to also teach the students, how they should behave in the presence of their bosses or pears. Quite often the parents also don't tell their children about the nitty-gritty of good manners. Just read this story to find how harmful it can be for one who does not observe the basic principles of manners in his office.

This story pertains to a Christian engineer who used to work under me at Bharat Heavy Electricals, Tiruchirappalli, a well known Public Sector Undertaking, as an Apprentice Engineer in 1960's. I was a Senior Engineer in the Industrial Engineering Department of the company. Though I was quite satisfied with his work, my boss was not happy with him. And would you like to know, why?

When I asked my boss about the reason of his displeasure he told me that this boy never used to wish him "Good Morning" when he used to come to the office in the morning. So I asked the boy why he didn't wish the boss "Good Morning". When I asked him about the reason, he told that he used to get up and wish "Good Morning" every day but when he used to wish him the boss always seemed to look in some other direction. But he used to sit down after wishing him "Good Morning." So the boss used to think that he had not wished him.

The boy used to wish him but his style was wrong.

The boss developed so much hate for him that he called me

and told me to spoil his Confidential Report to an extent that the company had no choice but to remove him from the rolls.

The boss told me that he would ensure that no one ever came to know that I had spoiled his Confidential Report.

On his assurance, I complied with his wishes even though I didn't want to do so. Based on the Report, the boy got terminated from the services even though the boy had got married just a few days back and had celebrated his marriage with his colleagues only a day back.

As this news spread, his colleagues told him that I could have not spoilt his Annual Report. Everybody knew me as a good hearted person. So nobody suspected that I could have spoilt the Confidential Report of the boy. They even asked my wife whether I had spoilt the Confidential Report. She asked me about it but I told her that it was not so. I denied to have spoilt his Report because my boss had assured me that nobody would come to know about it. Actually even my boss declined to have spoilt the Report. So, all Graduate Apprentices went to the Personnel Department to find out the reason for his termination. The moment they came to know that I had lied to them, they threatened me of dire consequences. I told the boss about this development. I told him that the engineers had threatened me of dire consequences. I was afraid that they could maim our one year old daughter. So he provided a security guard at my house.

Though they spared me as well as my wife and daughter, I know how petrified I felt for several months after this incident. I could take a breath of sigh only after I came to know that he had managed to secure a good job in some private company in a nearby city through the personal contacts of the father of one of the engineers.

Though he got a job soon after getting terminated, just imagine how much shocked he as well his parents must have felt when they must have learnt that he had been terminated from the services soon after his marriage.

Had it been a Hindu family, the parents of the boy would have perhaps asked the boy to divorce the girl saying that the girl was not lucky for the family. But neither the parents of the boy asked him to divorce the girl, nor the boy thought of divorcing the girl.

I have always been cursing myself for having spoilt his Confidential Report. I realized that I should have actually guided him that he should not sit down till he had ensured that the boss had seen him wishing in the morning instead of spoiling his Confidential Report. I had agreed to act on the instructions of my boss only because he was my boss.

But see how lack of manners can spoil one's career. Is it not more important to know how to behave with others than to become an engineer or a doctor?

21 *Life of Louis Braille*

There are so many handicapped persons who can also achieve the goals they may set for themselves if they have strong will power to achieve the goals. When we think of the people of this type the name of Louis Braille flashes immediately across our mind. He is known all over the world for the system known as Braille System. The blind persons can read any thing written in Braille system when they get conversant with the system. This story, however, tells about the type of problems he had to pass through to get recognition for the system. He can, thus, be an icon for all the handicapped persons.

The Braille system, as we know, uses different combinations of six dots protruding on the paper to represent all characters of the English alphabet besides various punctuation marks which the blind people can sense by touching the dots with their fingertips.

Louis Braille was born in 1809 to French parents. When he was born he had normal eyes like anybody else. His father was a harness maker and had a small shop where Louis used to go and play. When he was only three years old, one day he held two sharp awls and ran out of the shop. But on the way he stumbled and one of the awls pierced through his eye.

When the awl pierced his eyes, his father took him to a doctor but despite the best care available at that time, the infection spread to the other eye also which left him totally blind. But he had seen the world with his own eyes and was able to sense how deprived a person not having eyes would feel. It is this thought that inspired him to do something that could save the blind people from their feeling of deprivation.

Even as a child, after this incident, he evolved a system of telling his neighbours where he was going, by different number of tappings of his cane on the ground. But due to the dejection and frustration of having lost the vision of his eyes, he realized how dejected the people who were born blind must be feeling because of this handicap. So he kept on thinking of some way or another which could enable them to get rid of such a feeling.

At the age of ten, he first of all joined "Institution Nationale des Jeunes Aveugles" - a school for the blind in Paris where Valentine Hauy taught him the alphabets by guiding his fingers along the twenty-six letters of the alphabet made from twigs. After learning the shapes of the alphabet he started reading the books that were kept in the school's library, made up of letters cut out of cloth and pasted on the leaves of the books. But he noticed that even a small fable required six to seven big books prepared by this method, each weighing about eight pounds. Though the Institute improvised the books by using only about one-inch high, embossed letters instead of the letters made of cloth, but even this improvisation didn't appeal to Louis much. So he kept on thinking of some alternative method. Initially he tried to devise codes consisting of triangles, squares and circles to denote various characters of the alphabets. But this concept didn't satisfy him.

One day when he was sitting in the café of the Institution which he had joined as a teacher, he listened to the news that a French army captain Charles Barbier de la Serre had developed a system for tactile writing and reading using raised dashes and dots, which the soldiers could use in the field to compose and read messages even at night, without illumination. The system used simple army codes such as one dot for "advance" and two dots for "retreat". Barbier even adapted his system and presented it to the Institution for the Blind Youth, hoping that it would be officially adopted there. But his system used a 12-dot cell and was based on the phonetics. Taking a lead from this system, in about three years' time, by the age of 15, Louis evolved a system of his own - the system the world knows as "Braille System". His system used sixty three different combinations of only six protruded dots to represent various alphabets as well as various punctuation marks, the contractions and some small words like "and" and "for". He employed the tip of an awl to mark these protrusions which the blind people could touch with their fingers and feel what was written.

He paid homage to the great blind poet John Milton by preparing some sections of his poems in this system. He even demonstrated that he was able to "punch-write" in this manner almost as fast as anyone could dictate to him. This system has become so popular that nowadays many books have been written using his system for the blind people. So much so even the Harry Potter series of books is available in the Braille system.

But his senior colleagues labeled him as a cheat. They accused that he used to mug up the passages he chose to demonstrate. So when he proposed to the French Academy to include the system developed by him in the school as a curriculum, his proposal didn't get accepted. The authorities felt that the prevailing embossing system was good enough for the blind people.

It is an irony that people generally always oppose any new brilliant idea when it is proposed as happened in this case. Even Graham Bell had received a cold response from the President of the USA when he had talked to him over his phone to show how messages could be transmitted through wires and heard at the other end of the wire using an instrument without which life is impossible today.

Since his proposal had been turned down, Braille motivated some of his students to come forward and learn the system and taught them his system secretly. Apart from the language, he also taught them to punch out mathematical symbols and solve equations. He even evolved a Braille musical code and became a skilled organist.

But out of disappointment, Braille started losing his health gradually. It was not until one of his blind students gave a piano recital by listening to the Braille musical notes created by her companion by tapping on the table kept on the stage.

On receiving a hearty applause, addressing the audience she said. "Your applause is not for me. It belongs to a man who is dying." She then told the public about the educative and useful Braille method that had introduced a blind girl like her to the magic of music. She narrated how it was the jealousies of the older colleagues that had kept the system closeted and had thereby denied the horizon to millions of blind people all over the world. The crowd, charged with emotion, demanded acceptance of the Braille's system and the news made headlines. Gradually quite a number of Samaritan publishers started publishing books employing his system, for the blind.

Louis Braille was on his deathbed when the news of this success came to him. He was overwhelmed with joy and through tears rolling down his cheeks, he said, "This is the third time in my life I have permitted myself to weep. First when I was blinded. Second, when I heard about the army code for 'night-writing', and the third time now, because I know that my life has not been a failure". It was sheer good luck that he was still alive to get the news.

On his death, a bust of Braille was erected in recognition of his great contribution to the blind people of the world, outside the shop of his father at Coupvray, a small town near Paris where he was born. The sculptor has endowed the bust with eyes with so much compassion that they draw immediate attention of any viewer toward them.

He could have also remained unknown just like any blind person. But he had strong determination. He did not give up his efforts from the very day the awl pierced through his eye. He finally converted his grief into a system for which the whole world feels grateful to him. Whole credit goes to him for having made it possible for the blind people to read even newspapers printed using the Braille system.

We should take an inspiration from people like Louis Braille to make our life useful to others. But it would be better to develop a similar system for the other languages also. May be someday somebody would also fill the need of the blind people who don't know English.

22 Story of the Servant who Kept on Giving Pain Relieving Drops to Our Son

I shifted from the Tiruchirappali Unit of Bharat Heavy Electricals to its Ranipur Unit in 1971. My wife, who was working as doctor at the Tiruchirappalli Unit also shifted to Ranipur along with me. Both of us were going to get our time-scale promotions within a year or so. We both were very close to get our time-scale promotions at Tiruchirappalli. But we realized that it would be better for us to shift to the company's Ranipur Unit instead of continuing at Tiruchirappalli. So we filed an application for our transfer and got ourselves transferred from there.

However after we reached Ranipur we came to know that both of us would lose our seniority because as per rules of the company, anybody who sought transfer of his or her own accord would lose his or her seniority for the purpose of promotion. Had we known about this rule we could have asked for our transfer after getting promoted at Tiruchirappalli. To me, however, this rule appeared to be unethical because an employee who may have served an organization for a longer period should not be made to get a severer punishment than an employee who may be junior to him or her.

I represented my case and surprisingly our Head Office agreed to the plea taken by me.

But on the day this order was received from the Head Office at Ranipur, I had already submitted my resignation because I had been offered a job by Scooters India Limited, Lucknow. The Engineers' Union, therefore, asked the Personnel Department to do not disclose the contents of this order to me lest I should withdraw my letter of resignation.

So I joined Scooters India Ltd, at Lucknow and my wife also resigned after a week or so. But at that time our son was just fifteen days old. So we had to leave the child at some place so that she could go to Ranipur to hand over charge to some other doctor and get relieved.

Because we did not know anyone at Lucknow, we decided to leave the baby at Kanpur at my brother's house for three days till she came back from Ranipur.

I could have taken leave for a few days to also stay at Kanpur along with the baby when my wife was not there but a new employee can get only an unpaid leave till he earned some earned leaves by serving the organization for at least a few months. So it did not occur to me that I should have taken unpaid leave. But I did not know what tragedy was in the offing.

Though my brother is a doctor himself, to our great surprise he did not intervene when our teenaged girl servant whom we had left at Kanpur to look after the baby, started giving the baby "Baralgan drops" every time he cried. My wife had told her that she could give the baby these drops if he cried due to abdominal cramps.

Baralgan was a medicine my wife also used to give to the baby whenever he used to cry due to pain in his stomach. But she did not tell the servant that its overdose could be very dangerous. So she should not give it more than once or at the most twice a day. Since the servant did not know that the medicine should have not been given every time the child cried, she finished almost the whole bottle of the medicine within two days by the time we reached Kanpur to bring back the child and the servant. Due to the overdosage, the condition of the baby had deteriorated so much that he had started passing out the milk that was fed to him without retaining the milk even for a minute in his stomach.

By the time we reached Lucknow the condition of the baby became still worse. So much so, we even lost the hope of his survival. So we found out who was the best pediatrician of Lucknow. Every one told us that we should show him to the

Assistant Professor of the King George's Medical College. So we took the child to him. But the doctor told us to admit the child the next day instead of admitting him the same day. When we enquired about the reason, after great persuation he told us that if we admitted the child in the hospital that day, he would be admitted in the ward which is assigned to the Head of the Department and not in the ward assigned to him. When my wife told him that she was herself a doctor and asked him whether he thought the child could survive for one more day if not admitted immediately, he allowed us to get the child admitted the same day. He also assured us that he would take care of the child even though he would be going against the rules of the hospital.

Because our son had been admitted in the ward of some other doctor, we both went to the residence of that doctor also to explain the condition of the child. We fell down to his knees and requested him to save the child in whatever way he thought it could be possible. He prescribed such strong antibiotics that he told us he had not given so strong antibiotics to such a small child till then. Though he succeeded to save the child, we could not know at that time that the diarrhea had depleted some of the essential minerals the Mother Nature provides to a child at the time of birth, so that the child may have a healthy growth. We could come to know about this only when we sent our son to the school and we started getting complaints about his performance.

The Principal of the school where we had admitted the son was luckily of a very nice nature because she constantly guided us. She told us that we need not worry about his performance in the school. She consoled us by telling that the child would make us proud when he grew and she felt that he would do some extraordinary things in his life.

I have thought several times why I did not take unpaid leave and stay at Kanpur because had I been at Kanpur, even though I am not a doctor, may be I might have not allowed the servant to give the medicine again and again. May be the child was crying only because he did not see the mother around him and by finding me by his side, he would have not cried so often.

Actually we commit such mistakes only because we fail to take right decisions at such crucial occasions. We should hail those who are able to take correct decisions in their life as the successful people. Only the people, who take correct decisions, succeed in life more than others.

We should not think that such things happen because such things are destined to happen. If we think so, we only try to excuse ourselves of the mistakes we may have committed. We should not try to satisfy ourselves this way. A mistake is a mistake only. We come to know that we committed a mistake only after we have committed the mistake.

The lesson we can take from this story is that we should not mind taking "leave without pay" just in the interest of the office-work. We should give more priority to the family-interest. The very purpose of our working somewhere is to take care of the family. Anybody who gives more attention to the job than to his or her family is more liable to commit the type of mistake I had committed.

Though I had not taken three days' leave when we lodged our son at Kanpur at my brother's place, I had to take several days "leave without pay" when we admitted him in the hospital. I have even forgotten how many days' leave I had to take. But I have not forgotten how grave the mistake was.

23 *Our Miseries have no Tie-Up with Raahu Kaal or Ketu Kaal*

Raahu Kaal and *Ketu Kaal* are the periods during which some people hesitate to begin any auspicious work. They think that they can stave off their troubles by not taking any major decisions of life during *Raahu Kaal* and not starting journey to any new place during *Ketu Kaal.*

If we think so, only because our forefathers used to think so we should have a re-look at these beliefs. If we can take all necessary precautions we don't have to worry about these two *Kaals.*

In the past, a study seems to have been made to ascertain whether there is some cyclic pattern of the malefic periods to have arrived at a decision that we should take into consideration these two time-slots. However only in South India people take these findings seriously.

If you at all think logically, you would not give any significance to these time-slots. You would find that these concepts are fallacious. We don't have to go too far to look for the reasons to drop our faith in these time-slots.

The first fallacy in this concept is that there are no *Raahu Kaal* or *Ketu Kaal* during the nights as if no mishaps can occur during the nights. If we look at the incident narrated in the story of the Assistant Professor of geography and assume that the students whose answer-books had gone to this examiner had appeared for the examination during *Raahu Kaal,* we get confounded immediately by the thought that because all students had appeared in the examination at the same time, if some of the good students got poor marks there were many poor students who got good marks also. If the good students were affected by the *Raahu Kaal*, why the poor students were not affected by *Raahu Kaal*?

For the same reason, so many flights take off every day during the *Raahu Kaal* and *Ketu Kaal* from various airports. But mostly all of them reach their destinations without any problem as if they had not taken off during *Raahu Kaal* or *Ketu Kaal*? If the concept of *Raahu Kaal* had any relevance, all the airlines should think of rescheduling the take off times of their flights. Also they should even announce the *Ketu Kaals* so that the passengers do not board the flights during those hours. Actually they know these *Kaals* have no relevance. Particularly with the latest navigational technology in place there is no risk of any mishap in air. So the passengers do not think it risky to board the flights regardless of their take-off timings. The only thing some people keep in mind is the time of arrival of the planes at the destination. They do not select the flights which reach there during the hours of the months when the airport may be covered with dense fog.

By taking into consideration the *Raahu Kaals* or *Ketu Kaals* we can not save ourselves from committing mistakes or stave off mishaps.

In 2009, it was announced by the media that some company was planning to come out with wrist watches which would show *Raahu Kaals* on their dials so that people who want to avoid taking any auspicious decisions during *Raahu Kaal* may not have to calculate the *Raahu Kaals.*

Even the way of calculating these time-slots, can make one doubtful about these slots. The method of calculating these slots is therefore, being explained below.

These periods depend on the timings of the sunrise and the sunset which depend on the latitude and longitude of a place and the month of the year also.

The entire span between the sunrise and the sunset is divided in eight equal periods. Supposing on a particular day the time of sunrise is 6:00 a.m. and the time of sunset is 6:00 p.m. each period would start and end at the times given in the following tables on that day.

Periods of *Raahu Kaals*	Starting Time	Finishing Time
First	6:00 hrs	7:30 hrs
Second	7:30 hrs	9:00 hrs
Third	9:00 hrs	10:30 hrs
Fourth	10:30 hrs	12 noon
Fifth	12 noon	13:30 hrs
Sixth	13:30 hrs	15:00 hrs
Seventh	15:00 hrs	16:30 hrs
Eighth	16:30 hrs	18:00 hrs

Similarly the time-slots for calculating *Ketu Kaals* are, as follows:

Periods of *Ketu Kaals*	Starting Time	Finishing Time
First	1:30 hrs	3:00 hrs
Second	6:00 hrs	7:30 hrs
Third	7:30 hrs	9:00 hrs
Fourth	9:30 hrs	10:30 hrs
Fifth	10:30 hrs	12 noon
Sixth	12 noon	13:30 hrs
Seventh	13:30 hrs	15:00 hrs
Eighth	15:00 hrs	16:30 hrs

Once we have calculated these slots, we calculate the *Raahu Kaals* and *Ketu Kaals*, as follows:

Day of the Week	*Raahu Kaal*	*Ketu Kaal*
Monday	Second Period	First Period
Tuesday	Seventh Period	Sixth Period
Wednesday	Fifth Period	Fifth Period
Thursday	Sixth Period	Fourth Period
Friday	Fourth Period	Third Period
Saturday	Third Period	Second Period
Sunday	Eighth Period	Eighth Period

It may be observed that the First Period does not figure in the table of *Raahu Kaal* and the Seventh Period does not figure in the table of the *Ketu Kaal.* Also in the *Ketu Kaal* the fourth period starts half an hour late.

Now the question arises, should we knock off the *Raahu Kaal* and *Ketu Kaal* from our daily work-schedules? Each period lasts about one and a half hours. So it would amount to cutting short a day by about three hours every day.

Now just imagine, you have been called for an interview for a job during *Raahu Kaal.* Would you not go for the interview just because the time of interview falls during *Raahu Kaal*?

There are so many activities that we have to carry out daily in a perfunctory way. For example, we have to reach our office at some specific time only, everyday. Since the *Raahu Kaal*s are linked to the times of sunrise and sunset, can our office change the timings of the office on the month-to-month and calendar day-to-calendar day' basis? If the multinational companies were to follow this system, how difficult it would be for them to contact their counter parts or the executives working in the countries other than their own countries?

So it is even otherwise not practical to follow these concepts.

24 *Story of a Hairline Crack in Bone*

Though scientists have explored several secrets of Nature they have yet to find out several secrets that evade exposure. For instance, we still don't know what type of navigation system the honey bees use to come back to their own honey combs even after having flown sometimes two to three kilometers away from their honey combs to collect the nectar of flowers. They must not be recognizing the landmarks that may have fallen on their routes. Lobsters too go several kilometers away from their habitats but they also come back to their habitats. Under the sea the lobsters don't have even any ocean-marks of the type the bees can have on the land. So it is quite baffling how they come back to their habitats?

It looks there is some system about which we do not have much knowledge. This story also deals with an equally baffling instance.

This incident had happened in year 1982. My wife had her Nursing Home about 300 meters away from our house and she had to shuttle from the house to the Nursing Home as well as back from the Nursing Home to home at least seven to eight times every day. Sometimes she used to drive herself to the Nursing Home and back. Sometimes I used to take her to the Nursing Home. But very often she also used to go walking.

On a particular day, some gardeners had dug several pits in the park which is situated between the Nursing Home and our house, to plant trees. As she was not aware that they had dug pits in the park nor she could see the pits because it was quite dark when she was coming back from the Nursing Home, a leg of my wife slipped into one of these pits and she started limping. Though she reached home walking but she was not sure whether the leg may not have fractured. So to get rid of any doubt we went to one of the renowned orthopaedic surgeon of the city.

When we went to the surgeon, he took an X-ray of the leg and showed us the film. There was a thin line across the bone which he said appeared to be a hairline crack only. So he suggested that it would be necessary to get the leg plastered for about one and a half months.

We agreed to his suggestion and allowed him to plaster the leg. But when we reached home, my wife could not withstand the sight of plaster on her leg. She was worried, how she would go to the Nursing Home in this condition. She was also worried that she would have to also undergo physiotherapy for about a month after the removal of the plaster.

It was on one of these days only when a pundit whom we knew happened to visit us at home. He had no idea that my wife had fallen in a pit and she had got one of her legs plastered. He actually wanted some financial help for his son.

When we narrated him what had happened, he looked at the forehead of my wife and asked her, her birth day and the time of birth. He also saw the palm of my wife and then told us that according to astrology and the time when she had fallen in the pit there was absolutely no scope of any fracture in any bone of the body.

But because we had seen the X-Ray of the lower leg before we had allowed the orthopaedic surgeon to plaster the leg, we told him we could have believed him had we not seen the X-ray film which clearly showed a hair line crack in the bone.

When we told him that we had seen a crack in the bone, he said, "I am so sure about what I am telling that I would stop professing about the types of incidents can happen in the lives of people if it was proved that there was a crack in any of the bones of the body due to this incident."

We would have perhaps not even believed him had he not told me also something the same day about my stars also. What he told me took me by surprise at that time and I asked him, "How such a thing that he had told me could at all be believed by some one whose wife may be alive?" He again very firmly told me that I should again think carefully about what he had told because according to the positions of my stars and his calculations what he had told me could not be wrong. What he told me could have not been known not only to him but actually could not have been known to anybody except me and my wife. When I thought a little seriously I realized that the pundit was not at all wrong. This realization reassured us that he could be right in case of the fracture also.

He told us to take fresh X-ray to check that he was right. Looking at the confidence the pundit had evinced in his knowledge and his calculations we got the plaster on the leg cut open and got the leg once again X-rayed. You can imagine how happy my wife would have felt when we saw that X-ray film proved that the pundit was right.

So what would you say about the reliability of the Hindu system of astrology? It is a medieval system but we can't outright reject it.

But pundits only are able to tell us such astonishing things.

Of course there are many pseudo-pundits also. So you have to be very careful. These pseudo-pundits are just like quack doctors. They don't have any knowledge of the Hindu system of prophesying. They only guise themselves as pundits for the sake of money. So you don't have to believe just any pundit.

We did not go to the surgeon to tell him about the removal of the plaster. We only assumed that some hair may have fallen on the film when it was being washed in a tray in the open or when the film was being dried which the surgeon interpreted as a hairline-crack in the bone. But the Indian system of astrology came as a boon for us.

It looks that this knowledge that enables the pundits to tell such things is a branch of knowledge that has not been explored yet the same way as we have not yet been able to explore the type of the navigation systems the honey bees and the lobsters use.

We obviously can't depend on a technique that can't be documented and passed on to others. This knowledge is becoming extinct gradually because the people who possess it are not able to pass the knowledge on to the next generations. Or may be the possession of this knowledge expects one to have a high class pious life which people don't like to have these days.

25 *Story on Hiring Servants without Verifying their Credentials*

In November, 2009 the news of a working couple of Mumbai had appeared in the media which shocked the whole country. This couple had hired a lady to look after their small baby girl at their home when they were both away. This lady used to come at their residence about half an hour before they used to leave for their offices. But this lady used to drug their baby to make her drowsy and give her to a beggars' gang every day for which she used to get hundred rupees per day. This gang used to dress the child as a forlorn child and used to go out on streets for begging. The gang used to dress up the child again in her home-dress and hand back the girl at the home of the couple.

One day the mother of the child returned home a few hours ahead of her normal time and was shocked to see that this lady was watching TV in one of the bedrooms with her legs stretched over the bed. When she enquired about the child the servant broke down and told how she used to give away the child every day to the gang.

The couple was under an impression that they had made a good arrangement for the security of the child. But the mistake they had committed was that they had not verified the credentials of the lady before hiring her for this job. It is not known why they had not thought of keeping the child in some crèche. May be they did not have a suitable crèche near the place where they used to live. Quite possibly, they also did not have any elderly relative who could come and stay with them to look after the child. People did not have to face a problem of this type in the joint family system. But now people are forced to have a nuclear type of family and they have to manage somehow with these types of problems.

Here is one more incident that tells us why we should not hire servants without verifying their credentials. With more and more people needing the help of servants at home, the servants have become in short supply. So people get tempted to hire whatever type of servants become available to them. They feel satisfied that they could at least manage to get a servant and do not take the trouble of finding where they live. We too had committed a mistake of the same type in our life.

This is an incident of year 1998. Our son had taken the franchise of a famous software company of Delhi and had opened a Computer Institute in Hazratganj, a place often regarded as the Canaught Place of Lucknow. Because we had not recruited the senior faculty of the Institute yet, the parent company had sent one of their faculty-member to train the first Oracle-batch of the students. Though this faculty could have stayed even in some hotel, we thought, it would be courteous on our part to ask him to stay with us at our home itself. So we offered him to stay with us instead of letting him stay in some hotel during the period of this course.

But we had a serious problem during those days. Our regular servants had gone on long leave just before his arrival. So we sent out a word that we wanted to hire two or three servants for cooking food and to take care of other chores. We were very happy that somebody told us that three women staying in our neighborhood were looking for a job and could agree to work at our home. We were so badly in need of some servants that we did not have time to check where exactly they lived or to which place they belonged.

From their appearance and dresses we made out that they should be of some respectable families only. While one of them was a middle aged woman, the other woman a little younger to her, the third one was a girl of about thirteen years. We asked them to prepare a few dishes to ascertain whether they would meet our requirements or not. We were so satisfied with their cooking skill that we immediately hired them for a month because we expected our permanent servants to come back by that time.

Soon after the departure of the Visiting Faculty, we had to go to Dehradun to attend the marriage of the elder daughter of my younger brother also. These women had given so good service that we asked them to come back on job after our return from the marriage.

We came back from Dehradun on 25th June. After refreshing a little my wife went to the Nursing Home and the son went to his Computer Institute.

The next day when my wife returned from her Nursing Home, these women gave us a little porridge to eat and then a cup of tea. Though the porridge had a little different taste we did not suspect that the servants might have mixed some drug in it.

But they had mixed some drug in the porridge because by 4 p.m. we both had become unconscious. I was lying on my bed and my wife on her bed. From the Nursing Home my wife got a telephone call that she should come to the Hospital because an operation was going to start. After some time the hospital-staff again rang her up to find why she had not come to the Nursing Home. Since they did not get any response from her they sent a hospital-staff to our house. But as they told us later, one of the three servants was standing at the gate of the house and she turned away the hospital-staff telling her that she was taking rest. So the doctors could conduct the operation without waiting for her.

At about 7 o'clock they finished the operation and the doctors came to our house to find whether every thing was normal. They got shocked to find both of us lying unconscious on our beds and started giving us the necessary treatment. They did not find any of the servants in the house and kept on trying to save us for about three hours but we did not regain consciousness. By ten o'clock our son also reached home. Suspecting it to be a case of poisoning, they decided to rush us to the Medical College.

While we were taken to the Medical College, the doctors accompanied us to the College. They remained there for several hours and the news spread in the city like wild fire. We could not recover senses for two days. When we recovered we did not know what had happened to us. When we reached home we found that the servants had taken away all the jewelry that had been kept over a trunk in the box-room of the house. While they took away the jewelry they did not touch the cash that was also lying on the trunk.

Though we had thought of keeping the jewelry back in the locker of the bank on 25th itself, we were so tired that day that we thought we could as well keep the jewelry in the locker the next day. Little did we know that the next day could be even the last day of our life. We had not even prepared a Will yet. The son was still not well settled enough to earn for the family. But by the grace of God, we did not die. We however could feel that our return from the Medical College was no short of a miracle because we got one more lease of life.

My wife had purchased lot of diamond jewelry a week before we went to Dehradun. But whole of it got lost. Not just the jewelry of my wife the servants had taken away the jewelry of our daughter-in-law also. We would have not lost the jewelry had we not hired these servants without knowing their backgrounds.

We reported the matter to police and they found out that the servants had hired a room in the nearby colony only about a month back and had already left the room and gone away. Nobody had any more details about them. Only some of the neighbours told that they had seen a Maruti car standing outside our house that day and the servants seemed to have left with the stolen jewelry in that car only. But nobody had noted the number of the car.

Whatever happened to us can happen to any body else also. We never got back any of the lost jewelry. All we got was a lesson. We should have not extended the courtesy of offering the Faculty member of Delhi to stay at our house. Had we not thought of asking him to stay at our house we would have probably not hired these servants.

26 *Story of an Australian Lady who had Come to India for Spiritual Enlightenment*

If you want to travel to a country alone you should be cautious about the level of safety you could expect in that country so that you do not become a victim of some mishap of the type this Australian lady, who had come to India for spiritual enlightenment, had become.

This story relates to Dawn Emilie Griggs, a 59 years old Australian lady, who had arrived IGI Airport, New Delhi from Hong Kong, on 17th March 2004. As most of the international flights arrive the airport during midnight hours, her plane had also landed the airport at about 1 a.m. in the night. Keen to reach Jhandewalah as early as possible, she did not think whether it would be safe for her to travel alone during the night time or not. So after collecting her baggage, she hired a pre-paid taxi for Jhandewalah. Generally it is considered safe to travel by a pre-paid taxi in any country. But unfortunately it did not happen to be safe in her case.

The taxi would have hardly left the airport that the two drivers gagged her so that no one would hear her. After gagging her, they raped her and when she resisted they brutalized her by gouging out her eyes with a screwdriver and dumped her in a nearby field under a tree along with her belongings, after murdering her. Just imagine what type of torture the lady should have suffered when the drivers were trying to gouge out her eyes or the entire episode she had gone through.

Tourists come to a country hoping that the people of the country would present a good image of their country and bestow good respect to them. Though most of the people of Delhi know that it is unsafe for a woman to travel alone in a hired vehicle in the middle of night like this, the foreigners for whom traveling is safe in their countries may not be aware of the risk they may be taking by traveling at such odd hours in the other countries.

Even though she had come with such a good intention, her journey to spiritualism ended in such a macabre manner.

However just imagine had she cared to gather information about the level of safety women have in our country, when she booked her ticket, she would have perhaps not died this way. She would have not hired the taxi at such an hour. This tragedy would have not occurred had even her travel agent cautioned her to do not travel alone at such times from the airport to the city. The females have to be extra-cautious in our country, that too, if they are traveling alone. In winters they have to be particularly more cautious because all the roads leading from the airport to the city are usually very lonely after midnight.

The sad part of this episode is that this event happened in March, not during winter.

It is surprising that her destiny should have brought her all the way from Hong Kong to India to meet such an end.

Though the police of Delhi succeeded to arrest one of the culprits on the same day after scrutinizing the records of the pre-paid taxi booth of the airport and apprehended even the other offender within two months of the incident, such incidents are bound to create a feeling of insecurity in the minds of the foreigners who plan to visit our country. Actually this is not a lone incident of this nature. So many foreigners have been reported to have been molested and even murdered in so many cities.

We may anyway take a lesson from this incident that we should be cautious about our safety if we travel through a country or in a city where it may be risky to go alone by a hired vehicle from one place to another place.

27 *An Accident that Took Place on a Busy Road of Lucknow*

It is not necessary that we may get some punishment only when we ourselves commit a mistake. We may get punished for the negligence or mistake of others as well. The most common examples of such punishments are the negligence of the drivers of the trains or the pilots of the airplanes. People lose lives due to the mistakes or negligence of the drivers and the pilots. People may lose lives for technological failures of the equipments also.

In the month of June 2008, it was reported in the media that both pilots of an Air India flight had dosed off in the cockpit of the plane with about four hundred passengers aboard, on a flight from Jaipur to Mumbai. They had put the plane to fly in the auto mode before taking a nap. But the nap lasted a little too longer than they may have expected. So instead of landing at Mumbai, the plane overshot Mumbai and kept on flying for another half an hour or so. Just imagine what would have been the fate of the passengers had the plane met with an accident.

No passenger ever tries to check, how tired the pilots are, when they board a plane. What may happen after boarding is therefore, not in the hands of the passengers. It was again the zodiac immunity that held the command of all the passengers who had boarded that plane that day. There is very little a passenger can do to save himself or herself under such a situation. The airlines are supposed to ensure that they do not let the pilots who may be over-exhausted or may have boozed to take charge of the cockpits.

Who would have paid the price for the carelessness of the airlines had an accident taken place? But ironically such a thing can happen in any body's life in some form or another. No cash-compensation a transit-insurance cover may provide can ever support a family as much as its earning members can. It sometimes takes several years to get out of the miseries caused by such failures to the families of the people who get injured or who die in the air accidents or any other such incidents.

No one knows in advance when who may become a victim of such lapse or failures. When we get punished for the mistakes of others, it hurts us more than when we get punished due to our own mistakes.

Here is a story that narrates an incident of carelessness in the maintenance or timely replacement of the stays that hold the overhead high tension cables. At many places these cables cross over above the roads. If the stays of these cables are not checked periodically or are not replaced when their replacement may be due, these cables can fall over the underneath vehicles passing on the roads. The cars may get electrocuted and the occupants of the vehicles may get burnt for no negligence on their part, whatsoever.

The cables can snap any day if the stays become too weak to bear the load they support. If a mishap happens due to failure of a stay supporting the cables, who is to be blamed? No one knows on whom the cables may fall. Yet people keep on using the roads below such cables especially if these roads fall on their routes.

So to live or work in the areas where such risk is involved can be also deemed to be one of the attributes that makes us more prone to such hazards.

An incident of this type had occurred a few years back in Lucknow when an overhead high tension electric cable had fallen above some passers-by due to which they lost their life. But let's think why these people lost their lives. Had the Electricity Department been inspecting the condition of the stays holding the overhead cables periodically, perhaps this tragedy would have not occurred. Who was careless and who paid the price? Only those innocent people paid the price over whom the cable had fallen. Their only fault was that they were passing though the road at that time. However lots of people had passed just before the cable had fallen. They escaped the tragedy. Who saved them from the tragedy? They survived by mere stroke of luck.

In another case of the same type that had occurred in 2007 in Ghazaibad a 14 years old boy Shivanshu had come in contact with a 11,000 KV live wire that was hanging over the boundary-wall of the house where he was playing cricket along with his street-mates, when he climbed the wall. The boy had gone virtually in flames and even though his parents tried to save him, his one leg and one hand had to be amputated by the doctors. It was not a mere coincidence. It was also a case of callousness on the part of the Electricity Department, which had not visualized the chances of such an accident because the live wires hung at such a low height above the peripheral walls of the houses. The further story is however also quite interesting.

The Electricity Department gave a compensation of ₹ 2.5 lakhs to the boy's family. But the Department raised this money through donations from none else but the employees of the Department, in the form of their one-day salary.

As long as there are careless people in this world, we can't be sure when we may fall a victim to their carelessness. But God sometimes helps us. The next story narrates an incident that tells us, how!

28 *Story of a Newborn Baby Recovered from a Garbage Bin in Mumbai*

There are several incidents that establish that we pass through several incidents when we have a close shave with death but we don't die. We escape death sometimes due to our own intelligence and sometimes due to the intelligence of others. Sometimes even the circumstances help us to escape death.

I have myself passed through such occasions more than fifteen times. We only over certain time generally forget such incidents. I am narrating one of such incidents of my life which was quite a spine chilling incident of my life.

This incident happened at Bharat Heavy Electricals, Ranipur within a few months of my arrival at Ranipur from Tiruchirappalli plant when I was driving back from the Officers' Club of the factory just after midnight after watching a movie. My wife was sitting on the front seat by my side along with our three years daughter and our next-door neighbors were sitting on the back seat. It was when we were passing through a stretch of the road near the Main Hospital of the company that a leopard jumped from the right side of the road hardly six inches away from the front glass shield across the car. It was sitting by the side of the road and perhaps got frightened by the headlights of the car. But I still shudder to think what would have happened had it jumped only a split second late. Its paws would have torn my shoulders perhaps and I would have been lying in the hospital.

But we all get saved. I came to know that at some earlier occasions also such instances had occurred on this road. Who saved us? I think the destiny of some of the co-passengers. We did not get hurt because some body sitting in the car did not have to die yet.

This way sometimes we are saved by the destinies of others also.

There is a popular saying in Hindi "*Jako Rakhe Saian, Maar Sake Na Koi*" which means, "No one can kill one who is getting the protection of the Lord."

Here is an incident of this very nature that tells the truth of this saying.

This story had appeared in the media sometimes in July, 2007. The press reported that a poor mother dumped her newborn baby in a garbage bin out of her apprehension that she did not enough means to keep the child alive. The child made no efforts to save himself. Nor he could have made any efforts. Yet the child did not die.

It so happened that when a milk-vendor, who was going on his cycle to distribute milk to his clients in the Lokhandwala Complex of Mumbai in the West Kandivili early in the morning, he caught sight of some dogs pulling out something from a roadside garbage bin what looked like the body of an infant. As he looked into the bin he found it to be a one-day old newborn boy. When other passers-by saw the infant in this condition, they informed the police-post at Kurar, close to the complex. The cops of Kurar police luckily rushed the infant to Bhagwati Hospital at Borivili.

The police, after investigations, located a woman who admitted to have dumped the child in the garbage-bin. But she told the police that she had done so only out of abject poverty, because she was not in a position to look after the baby because of her meagre means. So many mothers dump their unwanted infants. Some parents do so if the child may have born out of an objectionable marriage or an illegitimate relationship also.

But this case got too much publicity because the child had no less than 26 stab-wounds on his body. These wounds might have been caused either by the poker type of iron-rod the rag-pickers carry with them to poke into the garbage bins to sense the type of garbage that may be lying in the bins.

The child was however, reported to have survived due to the medical care he received at the hospital, despite such a cruel treatment meted out to him. We have to imagine what could have happened had no one seen the dogs pulling out the child that day.

Definitely some invisible power should have come to his rescue. This power is invisible to eyes just like the data recorded on a compact disk. We can't read what is written on the disk through naked eyes. But we can listen to what is recorded on it by mounting it on a DVD player or a computer. The lesson we get from this story is that we need not fear death too much. We would not die a day before our death may be due.

Indian sages had suggested that some events of our life are dependent on the type of karma we may have done in the preceding life-cycles. But perhaps Nature has made a system that when we are born the memory of the previous life gets mopped out and we forget about our past life though in some freak cases it does not get mopped out fully. Such freak cases, though not too many, however give us some clue about the role our karma also play in our life. We of course keep on rewriting our destiny based on the karma of the preceding life-cycles through the present-life karma.

This is the reason why sometimes even the people who may have had excellent academic records also do not perform so well in their life as some of them who may not be academically so well qualified as they are. It is the choices people make about the opportunities that come their way that makes them perform better, not the academic qualifications alone. We however get enough opportunities in our life. Even if we miss some, we get some other opportunities also. So we should not become despondent. We should keep our spirits high always in hope that we would not miss the next opportunities as we missed in the past.

29 *Story of a German Farmer who Had Kept Lot of Money over the Kitchen Shelf*

This is an interesting story that tells why we should not be careless in our life. Every instance of carelessness may get translated into a loss as had happened in the case of this farmer.

We don't know what type of things may happen the next moment. Though this farmer had been able to recover the money he could have lost for ever it is not necessary that we may be also so lucky in our case. So it always pays to be careful.

This story relates to a German farmer Martin Rediberger of Rosenhelm. He had brought 10,000 Euroes in 100 Euro-denomination from the bank to buy a tractor but as he reached home, he left the money for a while in his kitchen and went to the adjoining room to answer a telephone call. No one generally expects any untoward thing may happen in such a short time. But while he was talking over the phone, his nanny goat Steffi entered the kitchen and stomached the currency notes one by one.

Though he may not have been away for more than a few minutes, by the time he came back, he was surprised to see that the goat had eaten almost all the notes except the last one, which was still in her mouth.

He was off for hardly five minutes or so. But sometimes such things can also happen. Though he realized the mistake that he should not have left the cash on the kitchen-shelf the farmer however immediately thought of contacting a Vet doctor to conduct an operation of the stomach to take out the money.

Just imagine what would have happened had the farmer not immediately contacted the Vet. By the next day the goat would have digested all the currency notes and he would have lost the money he had brought from the bank.

The important things to be watched in this incident are that had he kept the notes at a height, which would have been out of the goat's reach; the goat would have not been able to eat the notes. The other interesting thing in the story is that luckily he was able to see the last note still in the goat's mouth. Had he not been able to see it or had the goat gone out of the kitchen by the time he returned, he would have not been able to know what had happened with the notes. He could have, in that case, thought that some body had stolen the notes.

Quite often we keep things at a low height in hurry. If we are of a cautious type of person, we won't leave our cash like this in a room or in the office. The main thing that we learn from this story is that we should try to find out a solution to a problem that may arise in our day to day life instead of blaming the stars or our luck.

30 *Story of a Lewd Bureaucrat and His Daughter*

Children generally don't tolerate illegitimate relationships of their parents. Parents also don't want their children or spouses to know that they have illicit relations with some one. This story tells how shocked they feel when their children or spouses happen to know of such of their relations.

This incident had occurred in Lucknow about two decades back. This case relates to an IAS officer, who used to frequently go to a joint in Halwasia Market where people holding power in the Government used to be offered girls by the people who wanted some favours from them. In this case the bureaucrat had shot his own daughter dead in the joint.

It is said that this officer had one day, asked the owner of the joint to provide his own daughter to him. Though at that moment the owner did not express any dismay at this demand, he felt so hurt that he somehow managed to persuade the bureaucrat's own daughter to come to the joint at a time when he called the bureaucrat also. While the bureaucrat was very happy that the owner had agreed to offer his daughter to him, but he was shocked when he saw that instead of the owner's daughter his own daughter was waiting for him in the room. He could not control his temper when he saw his own daughter looking into his eyes.

His wife was not aware that her husband used to go to this joint, to enjoy girls. He was so frightened at the thought of the exposure of his character that he lost control and pulled out his revolver and fired two shots at his daughter out of the fear that she would go and tell the whole episode to her mother. The news shocked every one when it appeared in all the newspapers of the city.

We get a very good lesson from this story that we should not indulge in such activities that we may have to feel so much ashamed of ourselves when the matter may get exposed.

31 *Story of Lal's Pathological Lab*

This is an incident that shows how important is it to give unflinching support to the head of the family even when some such mishap may occur that may have brought his name to disrepute. Fidelity cements a marriage and infidelity undermines its stability.

Like every other thing human relations also fritter if we don't maintain them. The relations of the husband and wife depend on the mutual faith that they are loyal to each other. But situations may arise sometimes which may put our mutual faith to test. If at such moments also the wife and the husband don't suspect the integrity of each other it further strengthens their relationship.

Even if the public may think otherwise, the husband and wife have to show to the world that they don't share the views of the public. Public can't know so well about our spouse as we may know. So we should not repudiate the spouse ourselves.

Our mutual faith should not sink if we did not come across any instance of insincerity in the past. We should rather give all the moral support to the spouse that we can give at such junctures of life.

Marriage can break if we start doubting each other. But we should not start doubting each other even under flimsy circumstances.

This story tells how the solidarity of the family helps the husband or the wife at such occasions.

This incident had occurred in Delhi a few years back when the renowned pathological lab of the capital "Lal's Pathological Lab" had given an "HIV Positive Report" to a married person who was considered to be a very chaste person not only by his family but by his neighbors and friends also.

Just imagine how much tension this report may have created in his family. Even his neighbors were surprised when they came to know about this report. For his children this report came as a bigger shock especially because the news had appeared in all the prominent newspapers. They had always thought, their father had a strong character. But after this report got published in the papers, they were not able to stand erect on their legs in their schools in front of their teachers and classmates out of shame. Just imagine, how much this news must have shocked his wife.

But this man did not trust the report and he filed a case against the Laboratory and wanted the Laboratory to investigate its records. To save the reputation, the Laboratory took another sample of his blood and confirmed that the earlier report was wrong. But look at the trauma to which the family had already been exposed.

The family heaved a sigh only when the Laboratory publicly acknowledged the mistake by saying that due to some negligence in their Lab, his sample had got exchanged with the sample of somebody else, earlier.

Though many years have passed since then, this incident is still fresh in the minds of the people of Delhi because his whole family had very confidently asserted that the report could not be correct. Neither his wife ever doubted the character of her husband nor did his children ever doubt his character. So confident was the family that this report did not bring their relationships to brink. The marriage could have otherwise collapsed. But it did not collapse. Just imagine how great the husband would have felt when it was finally proved that even such a reputed Laboratory can give a wrong report sometimes.

Such a thing may not happen in our life. But we should take a lesson from this story that we should not let our faith in our spouse's character shake under such situations.

The reason of steadfastness of the relationship of a mother with her children is based on her knowledge that she had given birth to them. This knowledge makes their relationship permanent. In all other relationships only mutual sincerity can make the relationships permanent. So we should consider the past attitudes of the spouse before we ever raise a finger on his or her sincerity. We should evince our confidence in the spouse if he or she did not show any deviance in the past.

32 *Story of a Man who Wanted to be Sure before Blaming his Wife*

Though we can learn from the mistakes committed by others we can also learn from the mistakes others may not be committing.

This story pertains to an old man of about eighty years who had started frowning over his wife who, he found, had stopped giving him as much attention as she had been giving earlier. So instead of blaming her outright, he decided to consult an ENT specialist to find what was wrong with her. He went and told the doctor, who was also an octogenarian, "It seems my wife has become hard of hearing. She does not reply to anything that I ask her, these days."

The doctor advised him to first stand at a distance of 20 ft and put some question to her. If she did not reply, he told him to move closer and ask the same question from a distance of 15 ft. If she still did not reply from a distance of 10 ft also, he told him to move still closer to her and ask the same question from a distance of just 5 ft. If she responded, it was well and good. Otherwise he told him to come and meet him again.

The man asked his wife when she was working in the kitchen, "What is the menu for the lunch today?" He didn't hear any reply. So he moved closer to a distance of 15 ft and repeated the same question. But even now she didn't care to reply. Once more he tried after moving to 10 ft and then to 5 ft. It was only when he asked the question from a distance of 5 ft that he heard his wife telling him scornfully, "How many times do you want me to tell? I have already told you three times, 'Fish curry, rice and sambhar'." It was only then that he came to know that actually he had become hard of hearing, not the wife.

The lesson, we can take from this story is, "We should always verify the facts before blaming anybody."

We can avoid several misunderstandings if we adopt the habit of first checking our doubts before we doubt or blame some body.

33 Story of Warren Buffett's Second Marriage

May be due to a feeling of aloofness or whatsoever reason, it is seen that many of even financially well-off people sometimes don't lead a happy life. How aloofness enters their life? Even though they may not be short of money, but something makes them unhappy. The reasons may be quite diverse. Obviously they miss something in their life.

Whatever they may be missing, they can be happy if they have a family that may make them proud. The very assurance that we have somebody who would take care of us if we may fall ill or be in a pensive mood is enough to keep one's spirits high. In the autumn period of life, we feel the necessity of a companion of this type particularly if our children may be living in the countries or cities far away from our place of residence.

At such occasions one may feel the necessity of remarrying if his earlier wife may have expired. This can transform the autumn season of life into spring season. Of course such a step should be taken only if our children may have settled down in their life satisfactorily and may not be haunted by the idea of getting a step-motherly treatment at the hands of the new wife of the father.

The fact that a person as old as Warren Buffett could think of remarriage to have a partner of life cautions us why we should never misbehave with our present spouse. If we have good relations with our present spouse then only can we expect him or her to take care of us even if we may get paralyzed or may develop some other health problem in our old age. We should not forget it is only our spouse who can be at our bedside at all odd times, if God may forbid, something may force us to have an all time companion.

We have to understand that unless we have been sincere to our spouse during the prime part or the tough parts of our lives, why should he or she should be willing to share our troubles in the old age? This is the reason why we should remain faithful to each other in marriage despite all the temptations we may come across during our life. Everybody needs company of some body who may have tender feelings for us in his or her heart.

Only one to whom we may have been faithful can feel obliged to give us necessary company when we may need his or her company the most. The confidence that there is someone in this world whom we can rely that he or she will be with us, itself gives us a great relief. The children become too much occupied with their own jobs and with their own children. So we can't expect them to have enough time to spare when we may be ailing with a disabling disease. So if somebody's first spouse may have deceased and all the children may have been married off there is no harm in getting remarried to some one who may be sincere to us, for companionship. Men and women both need a companion in life. We feel too lonely if we don't have a companion. Even if we have everything in life if we feel lonely we do not feel happy. It is at such occasions that we come to know the advantages of having a true wife or a true husband. Only the wife or the husband can provide a lifelong company, not the children or the relatives.

The greatest value of marriage lies in the fact that we can't share all our problems and thoughts freely with anybody other than our wife or husband even though we may be quite friendly and free with him or her. The children have their own worries and ambitions. It is only the husband and the wife who can think to provide all types of company to each other. This is the reason why we have to have a wife or a husband even if we have everything in our life. It is because of this assurance why many people marry even when they may be in the seventies or eighties.

Warren Buffett has set an example of this type. He has made it clear to the world that relationships are more important than the money. Had it not been so why Warren Buffett, who has been reckoned as the second richest man of the last decade of the twentieth century, would have married as late as on his seventy-sixth birthday to a sixty years old lady Astrid Menks in 2007? She had of course worked as his office-companion for many years. So they both knew each other quite well. Moreover she was still single.

Buffett married her mainly for the sake of companionship only. His first wife Susan had died in July 2004 of a stroke at the age of seventy-two. He had tried to cope with the vacuum left by his wife in his life for three long years. But he came to a conclusion that no vacuum can be filled by anyone except a god natured spouse.

We should remember that some day we will also grow old like him and we would also need a companion like him. So instead of fighting with each other, we should try to resolve all the differences we may have with our spouse so that we may not have to look for some other spouse and discover that the earlier spouse was better.

Changing the spouse may not give us more happiness than a stable marriage can. It is therefore better to strengthen the marriage rather than weakening it through acts of betrayal.

We should not forget that there is no better investment in life than to have some companion who may be a company to us when we become old. This is the reason why we should not embitter the relationship by ridiculing each other for the things that are far less important than having a lasting relationship even if it may call for lot of mutual adjustments. We should at least not keep on focusing on the mistakes our spouse may have committed long back, say, even twenty or thirty years back. Re-echoing the past mistakes makes the relationship tense and unbearable. The best way to lead a happy married life is to evolve the habit of "Letting Be-gone, be Bygone".

We have to bear in mind; we can't ever find a person who may be perfect. So we should be content with the person whom we have married or the one who has married us and try to develop unison with him or her.

Marriage's biggest attribute is that it gives us enough opportunities to learn to live for somebody else. It gives us opportunities to adjust to somebody else's faults or weaknesses. It gives us opportunities to live in a manner that we may feel happy by making somebody else happy. It gives us opportunities to practice forgiveness because we have to essentially forgive the other person whom we have married, several times not just once or twice.

34 *Story of a Quack Doctor whose Patient Got Cured even by a Wrong Medicine*

This is a story of a quack doctor, who used to practice in 1950's in a small town of Uttar Pradesh, Khurja, where we used to live during those days. My father used to work in a bank located just above his clinic. Whenever I would go there I used to see almost a kilometer long queue of bullock carts with the villagers sitting over them who wanted to show themselves to the doctor for their illnesses.

This sight was an equivalent of the scene of the horde of cars we see these days at the multiplexes. This scene was an evidence of the popularity of this doctor even though he was not a qualified doctor.

As I know, this doctor used to keep about thirty to forty medicines in a cupboard of his dispensary, which had been "numbered" and he used to only write the number of these medicines in Urdu on the prescriptions issued to the patients. The patients used to take the prescriptions to his compounder, who used to dispense the medicines according to the numbers written on the prescriptions. After finishing his OPD the doctor used to check the medicine numbers written on the prescriptions.

One day the doctor became very nervous when he noticed that the compounder had read the number of a medicine written on the prescription upside down and given a medicine of wrong number to a patient. He thought that the patient would die because a wrong medicine had been given to him, instead of getting cured. So he lost his temperament and started slapping and abusing the compounder in front of every one. But every body got surprised when one day, the same patient came back and thanked the doctor for having cured him. The compounder recognized the man whom he had given the medicine of wrong number.

Even the doctor got amazed at this miracle. The patient got cured even when he did not get the medicine that he had prescribed.

How would you explain this phenomenon? It looks the mistake had happened because the patient could be cured only by the medicine that he had received not the medicine the doctor had prescribed.

May we see in this instance that there is some super power in the world which sometimes intervenes when we are about to commit a mistake? Do we call such intervention only "luck"?

We of course can't say whose luck had saved the patient: the doctor's or the patient's luck.

It is said. "Luck helps those people more, who don't depend on it." When the luck helps us, all circumstances get aligned in a manner that we do not face much problem in getting our work done. Sometimes we even get credit for the work that may have been done not by us but someone else. However can we depend on only luck always? Obviously, not! We have to make our efforts notwithstanding whether luck is going to help us or not.

35 Story of a Doctor who Died of Cancer Despite Having been Very Kind to His Patients

The theory of karma tells that if we help somebody who may be in dire need of some help, we may not necessarily be helped by the same person whom we may have helped but the chances are we may get help from some other person whom we may not have helped at all in our life when we may need some help. This theory tells us why we should not abstain from helping people who may be passing through some crisis.

Though it is also said that God helps the people who help others, it is not known why even the people who may have been helpful to others through out their life also contact diseases like cancer or Alzheimer's and suffer in their life. This story tells why we should not doubt the validity of this concept and why we should always help the people who may be in some trouble if we can.

This is the story of an orthopaedic surgeon Dr. Pran Gandhi, who had a Nursing Home at Panipat in Haryana. Every resident of this town knows, how much pains this doctor used to take particularly in case of the poor patients. He did not use to take even fees from most of them. Besides taking pains, he used to help them financially also.

Yet this doctor developed cancer in his pituitary gland and had to leave this world when he was hardly 57 years old.

Since the Theory of Karma tells that the Super Power that has created the universe rewards the person who may have not harmed or hurt any one in his or her life it is quite natural to wonder why this doctor should have got infested with an incurable disease like the cancer of the brain.

The occurrence of such cases, at the outset is bound to baffle anyone about the Theory of Karma. But actually the theory also has some corollaries. So we need not shake our confidence in the theory.

According to me, had the doctor not been treating the poor and the needy people on a charitable pattern, he might have perhaps died much earlier. But his good deeds helped him to have established his children in their life quite well before his death.

So God had actually rewarded him only for the good deeds he had performed in his life. May be he would have not been able to educate and settle his children so well as he was able to do, had he not looked after the poor patients from all over in such a noble manner.

We of course don't know what sort of system God may have evolved to keep a track of the good and bad deeds of the people. But for sure He may be having some system to balance the effect of our good and bad deeds. After all just a few years back we could have not thought it possible to write anything except writing on a paper with the help of an ink pen or a pencil. But now we are able to write almost everything on a compact disk or on a pen drive and are able to read it also on a computer. Are we not? There are so many mysterious things God has evolved. For instance, do we know what system God has evolved to let the eels emit such powerful electric sparks to kill their preys under the sea as they emit? We would need electricity generated in a power house and a transformer to emit such sparks. Won't we? But eels don't need a power house or a transformer.

If He could have evolved such a system for the eels, we should not get surprised if He may have also evolved some system to record our deeds to level them, which may be well beyond our present power of comprehension.